SUPE[illegible]

PRINCIPLES

U.S. Terrorism Against Cuba

Noam Chomsky
Howard Zinn
William Blum
Michael Parenti
Leonard Weinglass
Nadine Gordimer
and others
Edited by Salim Lamrani

Common Courage Press Monroe, Maine

Cover art by Matt Wuerker
Cover design by Matt Wuerker and Erica Bjerning

Library of Congress Cataloging-in-Publication Data is available from publisher on request.
ISBN 1-56751-340-9 paper
ISBN 1-56751-341-7 hardcover
ISBN-13: 9781567513400 paper
ISBN-13: 9781567513417 hardcover

Common Courage Press
121 Red Barn Road
Monroe, ME 04951

207-525-0900
fax: 207-525-3068

www.commoncouragepress.com
info@commoncouragepress.com

First printing
Printed in Canada

Contents

DEDICATION

To the Cuban Five
unjustly condemned

INTRODUCTION

The relationship between Cuba and the United States must be analyzed on the following clear basis: in today's world, relations between the various nations are not governed by right but by might. Terrorist violence has been the main engine of the relationship between the two countries.

In the history of international affairs, Cuba has been the country which has suffered from the longest terror campaign, orchestrated by the greatest world power. There is no other possible comparison, and this axiom would be known by all if there were even the slightest attachment to the facts.

Since 1959 the Cuban population has lived under a permanent state of siege which has conditioned its way of life. The range of methods used is impressive: direct military invasion, biological attacks, terrorist warfare, sabotage of infrastructures, assassination campaigns, economic strangulation, propagandist war and constant political and diplomatic aggression.

Far from belonging to the Cold War framework, the doctrine, which consists of imposing on the Cuban Revolution conditions intended to lead it to its complete annihilation, is still in force. In May 2004, the Bush administration increased the economic sanctions, which seriously affect the health of the most vulnerable: women, children and elderly people. In the name of an anti-revolutionary and obscurantist hostility Washington is determined to starve a whole population, by drawing upon a fallacious concept of "democracy".

It would be proper to wonder whether financing paramilitary attacks against the Cubans, as the U.S. government has been doing for more than forty-five years, has the aim of setting up the rule of law. Would it be possible "to restore democracy" by practicing terrorism? Does conducting a propaganda campaign consisting of the darkest deceptions about Cuba's problems and displaying an obvious scorn towards the truth and international opinion, have so noble a goal?

The war against terrorism, as carried out by Washington, has a variable geometry. Indeed, it is carried out only against the groups that do not serve U.S. hegemonic interests. The case of five Cuban political prisoners shows this without any possible ambiguity. Risking their existence, Gerardo Hernández Nordelo, Ramón Labañino Salazar, Antonio Guerrero Rodríguez, Fernando González Llort and René González Sehweret infiltrated the extremist clans of the Cuban exiles in Florida, people responsible for several hundreds of attacks against the Cuban population. Supported by irrefutable evidence, the Cuban government then informed the FBI of the criminal activities of the Miami fanatics. In response, the Five were condemned to four life sentences, plus 77 years of loss of liberty.

Several internationally renowned authors, Ricardo Alarcón, William Blum, Noam Chomsky, Piero Gleijeses, Nadine Gordimer, Saul Landau, Gianni Minà, Michael Parenti, James Petras, Michael Steven Smith, Ignacio Ramonet, Jitendra Sharma, Wayne S. Smith, Leonard Weinglass and Howard Zinn, whose dedication to all progressive and just causes across the entire world is known to all, agreed to take part in this collective work as soon as they became aware of it. The sixteen texts try to throw light on the complex Cuban question and the roots and objectives of American foreign policy since the end of the 18th century. Terrorism is a plague especially when practiced by the major world power, which also allows itself to condemn to life sentences heroic self-effacing people who risked their lives to forestall atrocities like those committed on September 11, 2001 against innocent civilians.

The aim of this work is to show the truth to the American people and the international community and to reveal the cruelties committed by Washington against Cuba. In the past, Americans have always shown that they are able to support generous causes providing they escape the powerful disinformation and indoctrination machine created by the Information multinationals. The ambition of this modest project is to offer to the public the historical tools necessary to formulate a judgment on one of the most anachronistic and cruel aspects of U.S. foreign policy.

Asserting the right of the Cuban people to control their destiny and live in liberty and peace, is more than a praiseworthy action, it is a pressing and urgent obligation. Fighting for the release of the Five is more than a noble act, it is a necessary and basic duty.

—Salim Lamrani

PART A

U.S. TERRORISM AGAINST CUBA

CHAPTER ONE

HOWARD ZINN

Howard Zinn grew up in Brooklyn and worked in the shipyards before serving as an air force bombardier in World War II. Zinn was chair of the history department at Spelman College, where he actively participated in the civil rights movement, before taking a position at Boston University.

Howard Zinn is professor emeritus at Boston University. He is the author of the classic *A People's History of the United States*, "a brilliant and moving history of the American people from the point of view of those...whose plight has been largely omitted from most histories" (Library Journal), and "a shotgun blast of revisionism that aims to shatter all the comfortable myths of American political discourse" (Los Angeles Times). A television adaptation of *A People's History of the United States* is currently being co-produced by Matt Damon, Ben Affleck, and Chris Moore for HBO.

Zinn has received the Thomas Merton Award, The Upton Sinclair Award, the Lannan Foundation Literary Award for Nonfiction and the Eugene V. Debs award for his writing and political activism.

Zinn is the author of numerous books, including *Declarations of Independence*, *The Zinn Reader*, the autobiographical *You Can't Be Neutral on a Moving Train*, *Terrorism and War on September 11 2001*, and the play *Marx in Soho*.

He now lives with his wife, Roselyn, in Massachusetts and lectures widely on history and contemporary politics.

The Roots of United States Policy Toward Cuba

When the United States, after a series of military expeditions, pushed Spain out of Florida, in 1819, in an operation euphemistically called the "Florida Purchase" the island of Cuba came into view. Four years later, the United States government announced to the world "The Monroe Doctrine", which made it plain to the nations of Europe that the United States considered itself the protector of the Western Hemisphere.

The year of the Monroe Doctrine, 1823, Thomas Jefferson, whose presidency had ended fifteen years earlier, wrote to President James Monroe:

"I candidly confess that I have ever looked on Cuba as the most interesting addition which could ever be made to our system of States. The control which, with Florida point, this island would give us over the Gulf of Mexico, and the countries and isthmus bordering on it, as ell as those whose waters flow into it, would fill up the measure of our political well-being."

Jefferson added, however, that this would require a war, which he did not favor.

Seventy five years after Jefferson's letter to Monroe, in the year 1898, the war he rejected took place, the result of which was to place Cuba under the control of the United States.

In the schools of the United States, the first mention of Cuba comes when classes take up the "Spanish-American War". This same war was retitled by the Marxist historian Philip Foner as the "Spanish-Cuban-American War". The difference in the two names gives a clue to the fact that there are two fundamentally different points of view about the war of 1898. In one of them the Cubans are missing. In the other, they are a critical presence.

Only with the war of 1898 are American students (I use the adjective ”American”, but it should be understood that this refers to he United States, where there is no corresponding term for the more accurate Spanish word “estadounidense”) introduced to the idea that their nation sends military forces into other countries. Indeed, it is shortly after that war that the expression “America as a world power” becomes generally used.

However, long before the war in Cuba, the United States was sending military forces into other countries, not only in Latin America but as far away as West Africa, Japan, China. In 1962, Secretary of State Dean Rusk, trying to justify the attempt by the United States to invade Cuba in the Bay of Pigs told a Senate Committee, there were precedents for the use of armed force against Cuba, and gave the committee a State Department list which showed 103 military interventions between 1 798 an 1895.

For instance, in 1854 the American government ordered the destruction of the city of San Juan del Norte, as retaliation for an “insult” to the American minister of Nicaragua. And the following year, United States and European forces landed in Uruguay, in the words of the State Department “to protect American interests during an attempted revolution in Montevideo.”

Thus, by the 1890s, there had been much experience in military interventions overseas. The ideology of expansion was widespread in the upper circles of military men, politicians, businessmen—and even among some of the leaders of farmers' movements who thought foreign markets would help them.

Captain A.T. Mahan of the United States navy, a popular propagandist for expansion, greatly influenced Theodore Roosevelt and other American leaders. The countries with the biggest navies would inherit the earth, and “Americans must now begin to look outward", he said.

Henry Cabot Lodge, Senator from Massachusetts wrote in a magazine article:

`In the interests of our commerce...we should build the Nicaragua canal, and for the protection of that canal and for the sake of our commercial supremacy in the Pacific, we should control the Hawaiian islands and maintain our influence in Samoa...and when the Nicaraguan canal is built, the island of Cuba...will become a necessity.... The great nations are rapidly absorbing for their future expansion and their present defense all the waste places of the earth. It is a movement which makes for civilization and the advancement of the race. As one of the great nations of the world the United States must not fall out of the line of march."

On the eve of the war in Cuba, there was an editorial in the Washington Post:

"A new consciousness seems to have come upon us—the consciousness' of strength—and with it a new appetite, the yearning to show our strength.... Ambition, interest, land hunger, pride, the mere joy of fighting, whatever it may be, we are animated by a new sensation. We are face to face with a strange destiny. The taste of Empire is in the mouth of the people even as the taste of blood in the jungle...."

If indeed there was such a taste in the mouth of some people (there was no way of telling how widespread this was) it was certainly created, encouraged, advertised and exaggerated by the millionaire press, the military, the government, the eager-to-please scholars of the time. Political scientist John Burgess of Columbia University said that the Teutonic and Anglo-Saxon races were "particularly endowed with the capacity for establishing national states...they are entrusted...with the mission of conducting the political civilization of the modern world."

Several years before his election to the presidency, William McKinley had said: "we want a foreign market for our surplus products." Senator Albert Beveridge of Indiana in early 1897 declared: American factories are making more than the American people can use; American soil is producing more than they can consume. Fate has written our policy for us; the trade of the world must and shall be ours."

These expansionist military men and politicians were in touch with one another. One of Theodore Roosevelt's biographers tells us: "By 1890, Lodge, Roosevelt, and Mahan had began exchanging views" and they tried to get Mahan off sea duty "so that he could continue full-time his propaganda for expansion."

Theodore Roosevelt told the Naval War College "All the great masterful races have been fighting races.... No triumph of peace is quite so great as the supreme triumph of war." And in the year 1897, not long before the war in Cuba, Roosevelt wrote to a friend: "In strict confidence.... I should welcome almost any war, for I think this country needs one."

Roosevelt was contemptuous of races and nations he considered inferior. When a mob in New Orleans lynched a number of Italian immigrants. Roosevelt wrote his sister that he thought the lynching was "rather a good thing" and told her he had said as much at a dinner with "various dago diplomats...all wrought up by the lynching."

William James, the philosopher, who became one of the leading anti-imperialists of his time, wrote about Roosevelt t hat he "gushes over war as t he ideal condition of human society, for the manly strenuousness which it involves, and treats peace as a condition of blubberlike and swollen ignobility, fit only for huckstering weaklings, dwelling in gray twilight and heedless of the higher life...."

By the year 1898, Cuban rebels had been fighting their Spanish conquerors for three year in an attempt to win independence. By that time, it was possible to create a national mood for intervention.

It seems that the business interests of the nation did not at first want military intervention in Cuba. American merchants did not need colonies or wars of conquest if they could just have free access to markets. The idea of an "open door" became the dominant theme of American foreign policy at the start of the twentieth century. It was a more sophisticated approach to imperialism than the traditional empire building of Europe.

But, if peaceful imperialism turned out to be impossible, it was always understood, military action might be needed. By 1898, a turnabout in the attitudes of U.S. business was taking place. There was already a substantial economic interest in the island, which President Grover Cleveland summarized in 1896:

"It is reasonably estimated that a least $30,000,000 to $50,000,000 of American capital are invested in the plantations and in railroad, mining and other business enterprises on the island. The volume of trade between the United States and Cuba, which in 1889 amounted to about $64,000,000 rose in 1893 to about $103,000,000."

There was popular support in the United States for the Cuban revolution, based on the thought that they, like thc Americans of 1776, were fighting a war for their own liberation. The United States government, however, the conservative product of its own revolution, had power and profit in mind as it observed the events in Cuba. Neither Cleveland, President during the first years of the Cuban revolt, nor McKinley, who followed, recognized the insurgents officially as belligerent. Such legal recognition would have enabled the United States to give aid to the rebels without sending an army. But there was fear that the rebels would win on their own and keep the United States out.

There seems also to have been another kind of fear. The Cleveland administration said a Cuban victory might lead to "the establishing of a white and a black republic" since Cuba had a mixture of the two races. And the black republic might be dominant. This idea was expressed in 1896 in an article in *The Saturday Review* by a young and eloquent imperialist, whose mother was American and whose father was English. This was Winston Churchill. He wrote that while Spanish rule was bad and the rebels had the support of the people of Cuba, it would be better for Spain to keep control. Churchill wrote:

"A grave danger represents itself. Two-fifths of the insurgents in the field are Negroes. These men...would, in the vent of success, demand a predominant share in the government of the country... the result being, after years of fighting, another black republic."

The reference to "another" black republic meant Haiti, whose revolution against France in 1803 had led to the first nation run by blacks in the New World. Churchill's fear was echoed by the Spanish minister to the United States, who wrote to the U.S. Secretary of State:

"In this revolution, the Negro element has t he most important part. Not only the principal leaders are colored men, but at least eight-tenths of their supporters.... and the result of the war, if the Island can be declared independent, will be a secession of the black element and a black Republic."

As Philip Foner wrote in his two-volume study *The Spanish-Cuban-American War*: "The McKinley Administration had plans for dealing with the Cuban situation, but these did not include independence for the island." He points to the administration's instructions to its minister to Spain, Stewart Woodford, asking him to try to settle the war because it "injuriously affects the normal function of business, and tends to delay the condition of prosperity" but not mentioning freedom and justice for the Cubans.

Foner explains the rush of the McKinley administration into war (its ultimatum gave Spain little time to negotiate) by the fact that "if the United States waited too long, the Cuban revolutionary forces would emerge victorious, replacing the collapsing Spanish regime"

In February, 1898, the U.S. battleship Maine, in Havana harbor as a symbol of American interest in the Cuban events, was destroyed by a mysterious explosion and sank, with the loss of 268 men. There was no evidence ever produced on the cause of the explosion [until the 1970s, when an official government investigation found the cause of the explosion to be a structural failure in the ship's engines], but excitement grew swiftly in the United States, and McKinley began to move in the direction of war.

The historian Walter Lafeber has written:

"The President did not want war; he had been sincere and tireless in his efforts to maintain the peace. By mid-March, however he was beginning to discover that, although he did not want war, he did want what only a war could provide; the disappearance of the terrible uncertainty in American political and economic life, and a solid basis from which to resume the building of the new American commercial empire."

At a certain point in that spring of 1898, both McKinley and the business community began to that their object, to get Spain out of Cuba, could not be accomplished without war. They also saw that their accompanying object, the securing of American military and economic influence in Cuba, could be ensured only by U.S. intervention.

The New York *Commercial Advertiser*, at first against war, by March 10 asked intervention in Cuba for "humanity and love of freedom, and above all, the desire that the commerce and industry of every part of the world shall have full freedom of development in the whole world's interest."

Congress by this time had passed the Teller Amendment, pledging the United States not to annex Cuba. It was initiated and supported by those people who were interested in Cuban independence and opposed to American imperialism, but also by business people who saw the "open door" as sufficient and military intervention unnecessary. But by the spring of 1898, the business community had developed a hunger for action. The *Journal of Commerce* said: "The Teller amendment...must be interpreted in a sense somewhat different from that which its author intended it to bear."

There were special interests who would benefit directly from a war. In Pittsburgh, center of the iron industry, the Chamber of Commerce advocated force, and the *Chattanooga Tradesman* said that the possibility of war "has decidedly stimulated the iron trade." It also noted that "actual war would very decidedly enlarge the business of transportation." In Washington, I was reported that a "belligerent spirit" had infected the Navy Department, encouraged "by the contractors for projectiles, ordnance, ammunition and other supplies, who have thronged the department since the destruction of the *Maine*"

Russell Sage, the banker, said that if war came: "There is no question as to where the rich men stand." A survey of businessmen said that John Jacob Astor, William Rockefeller, and Thomas Fortune Ryan were "feeling militant". And the leading banker J.P. Morgan believed that further talk with Spain would accomplish nothing.

On March 21, 198, Henry Cabot Lodge wrote McKinley a long letter, saying he had talked with "bankers, brokers, businessmen, editors, clergymen and others" in Boston, Lynn, and Nahant, and "everybody", including "the most conservative classes" wanted the Cuban question "solved". Lodge reported on his conversations: "They said for business one shock and then an end was better than a succession of spasms such as we must have if this war in Cuba went on."

On March 25, a telegram arrived at the White House from an adviser to McKinley, saying: "Big corporations here now believe we will have war. Believe all would welcome it as relief to suspense." Two days after getting this telegram, McKinley presented an ultimatum to Spain, demanding an armistice in the war between Spain and the Cuban rebels.

A spokesman for the Cuban rebels, part of a group of Cubans in New York, interpreted McKinley's ultimatum to mean the United States simply wanted to replace Spain in Cuba. He said:

"In the face of the present proposal of intervention without previous recognition of independence, it is necessary for us to go a step farther and ay that we must and will regard such intervention as nothing less than a declaration of war by the United States against the Cuban revolutionists….".

Indeed, when McKinley asked Congress for war on April 11, he did not recognize the rebels as belligerents or ask for Cuban independence. Nine days later, Congress, by joint resolution, gave McKinley the power to intervene. When American forces moved into Cuba, the rebels welcomed them, hoping the Teller Amendment would guarantee Cuban independence.

Many histories of the Spanish-American war have said that "public opinion" in the United States led McKinley to declare war on Spain and send forces to Cuba. True, certain influential newspapers had been pushing hard, even hysterically. And many Americans, seeming the aim of intervention as Cuban independence—and with the Teller Amendment as guarantee of this intention—supported t he idea.

But it is doubtful that McKinley would have gone to war because the press and some portion of the public (there were no public opinion surveys at that time) supported military intervention. It was the urging of the business community that was decisive. Several years after the Cuban war, the chief of the Bureau of Foreign Commerce of the Department of Commerce wrote about that period:

"Underlying the popular sentiment, which might have evaporated in time, which forced the United States to take up arms against Spanish rule in Cuba, were our economic relations with the West Indies and the South American republics.... The Spanish-American War was but an incident of a general movement of expansion which had its roots in the changed environment of an industrial capacity far beyond our domestic powers of consumption. It was seen to be necessary for us not only to find foreign purchasers for our goods, but to provide the means of making access to foreign markets, easy, economical and safe."

American labor unions had sympathy for the Cuban rebels as soon as the insurrection against Spain began in 1895. But they opposed American expansionism. Despite the feeling for the Cuban rebels, a resolution calling for U.S. intervention was defeated at the 1897 convention of the American Federation of Labor, whose president, Samuel Gompers, wrote to a friend: "The sympathy of our movement is genuine, earnest, and sincere, but this does not for a moment imply that we are committed to certain adventurers who are apparently suffering from Hysteria...."

When the explosion of the *Maine* in February led to excited calls for war in the press, the monthly journal of the International Association of Machinists agreed it was a terrible disaster, but it noted that the deaths of workers I industrial accidents drew no such national clamor. It said that the "carnival of carnage that takes place every day, month and year in the realm of industry, the thousands of useful lives that are annually sacrificed to the Moloch of greed, the blood tribute paid by labor to capitalism, brings forth no shout for vengeance and reparation...

The official organ of the Connecticut American Federation of Labor also warned about the hysteria worked up by the sinking of the *Maine*:

"A gigantic...and cunningly-devised scheme is being worked ostensibly to place the United States in the front rank as a naval and military power. The real reason is that the capitalists will have the whole thing, and when any workingmen dare to ask for the living wage, they will be shot down like dogs in the streets."

Some unions, like the United Mine Workers, called for U.S. intervention after the sinking of the *Maine*. But most were against the war. The treasurer of the American Longshoremen's Union, Bolton Hall, wrote "A Peace Appeal to Labor" which was widely circulated:

"If there is a war, you will furnish the corpses and the taxes, and others will get the glory. Speculators will make money out of it—that is, out of you. Men will get high prices for inferior supplies, leaky boats, for shoddy clothes and pasteboard shoes, and you will have to pay the bill, and the only satisfaction you will get is the privilege of hating your Spanish fellow-workmen, who are really your brothers and who had as little to do with the wrongs of Cuba as you have."

Socialists opposed the war. One exception was the Jewish *Daily Forward*. But *The People*, newspaper of the Socialist Labor party, called the issue of Cuban freedom "a pretext" and said the government wanted war to "distract the attention of the workers from their real interests." The *Appeal to Reason*, the chief Socialist newspaper, said the movement for war was "a favorite method of rulers for keeping the people from redressing domestic wrongs." In a San Francisco labor newspaper one Socialist wrote: "It is a terrible thing to think that the poor workers of this country should be sent to kill and wound the poor workers of Spain merely because a few leaders may incite hem to do so."

But after war was declared, Philip Foner says, "the majority of the trade unions succumbed to the war fever" Samuel Gompers called the war "glorious and righteous" and claimed that 250,000 trade unionists had volunteered for military service. The United Mine Workers pointed to higher coal prices as a result of the war and said: "The coal and iron trades have not been so healthy for some years past as at present."

The war brought more employment and higher wages, but also higher prices. Although Gompers was publicly for the war, privately he pointed out that the war had led to a 20 Percent reduction of the purchasing power of workers' wages. The Chicago *Labor World* said: "This has been a poor man's war—aid for by the poor man. The rich have profited by it, as they always do."

The prediction made by longshoreman Bolton Hall, of wartime corruption and profiteering turned out to be remarkably accurate. Richard Morris" *Encyclopedia of American History* gives startling figures:

"Of the more than 274,000 officers and men who served in the army during the Spanish-American War and the period of demobilization, 5,462 died in the various theaters of operation and in camps in the U.S. Only 379 of the deaths were battle casualties, the remainder being attributed to disease and other causes."

Thousands of soldiers got food poisoning. In May of 1898, Armour and Company, the big meatpacking company of Chicago, sold the army 500,000 pounds of beef which had been sent to Liverpool a year earlier and had been returned. Two months later, an army inspector tested the Armour meat, which had been stamped and approved by an inspector of the Bureau of Animal Industry, and found 751 cases containing rotten meat.

The Spanish forces were defeated in three months, in what John Hay, he American Secretary of State, later called "a splendid little war." The American military pretended that the Cuban rebel army did not exist. When the Spanish surrendered, no Cuban was allowed to confer on the surrender, or to sign it. General William Shafter said no armed rebels could enter the city of Santiago, and told the Cuban rebel leader, General Calixto Garcia that the old Spanish civil authorities, not Cubans, would remain in charge of the municipal offices in Santiago.

American historians have generally ignored the role of the Cuban rebels in the war; Philip Foner, in his history, was the first to print Garcia's letter of protest to General Shafter:

"I have not been honored with a single word from yourself

informing me about the negotiations for peace or the terms of the capitulation by the Spaniards.... when the question arises of appointing authorities in Santiago de Cuba...I cannot see but with the deepest regret that such authorities are not elected by the Cuban people, but are the same ones selected by the Queen of Spain...."

"A rumor too absurd to be believed, General, describes the reason of your measures and of the orders forbidding my army to enter Santiago for fear of massacres and revenge against the Spaniards. Allow me, sir, to protest against even the shadow of such an idea. We are not savages ignoring the rules of civilized warfare. We are a poor, ragged army, as ragged and poor as the army of your forefathers in their noble war for independence...."

Along with the American army in Cuba, came American capital. Foner writes:

"U.S. business interests set4 out to make their influence felt. Merchants, real estate agents, stock speculators, reckless adventurers, and promoters of all kinds of get-rich schemes flocked to Cuba by the thousands. Seven syndicates battled each other for control of the franchises for the Havana Street Railway, which were finally won by Percival Farquhar, representing the Wall Street interests of New York. Thus, simultaneously with the military occupation began...commercial occupation."

The *Lumbermen's Review*, organ of the lumber industry, said in the midst of the war: "The moment Spain drops the reigns of government in Cuba...the moment will arrive for American lumber interests to move into the island for the products of Cuban forests. Cuba still possesses 10,000,000 acres of virgin forest abounding in valuable timber...nearly every foot of which would be saleable in the United States and bring high prices."

Americans began taking over railroad, mine and sugar properties when the war ended. In a few years, $30 million of American capital was invested. United Fruit moved into the Cuban sugar industry, buying up 1,900,000 acres of land for about twenty cents an acre. The American Tobacco Company arrived. By the end of the occupation, in 1901, Foner estimates that at least 80 percent of the exports of Cuba's miners were in American hands, mostly Bethlehem Steel.

During the military occupation a series of strikes took place. In September 1899, a gathering of thousands of workers in Havana launched a general strike for the eight-hour day, saying: "...we have determined to promote the struggle between the worker and the capitalist. For the workers of Cuba will no longer tolerate remaining in total subjection."

The American General William Ludlow ordered the mayor of Havana to arrest eleven strike leaders, and U.S. troops occupied railroad stations and docks. Police moved through the city breaking up meetings. But the economic activity of the city had come to a halt. Tobacco workers, printers, bakers, went on strike. Hundreds of strikers were arrested, and some of the imprisoned leaders were intimidated into calling for an end to the strike.

The United States did not annex Cuba. But a Cuban Constitutional Convention was told that the United Stats army would not leave Cuba until the Platt Amendment, passed by Congress in February 1901, was incorporated into the new Cuban Constitution. The Platt Amendment gave the United States "the right to intervene for the preservation of Cuban independence, the maintenance of a government adequate for the protection of life, property, and individual liberty...." It also provided for the United States to get coaling or naval stations at certain specified points. The military bases at Guantanamo were given to the United States with no time limit.

The Teller Amendment and the talk of Cuban freedom before and during the war had led many Americans—and Cubans—to expect genuine independence. The Platt Amendment was now seen, not only by the radical and labor press, but by newspapers and groups all over the United States, as a betrayal. A mass meeting of the American Anti-Imperialist League at Faneuil Hall denounced it, ex-governor George Boutwell saying: "In disregard of our pledge of freedom and sovereignty to Cuba we are imposing on that island conditions of colonial vassalage."

In Havana, a torchlight procession of fifteen thousand Cubans marched on the Constitutional Convention, urging its members to reject the Platt Amendment. But General Leonard Wood, head of the occupation forces, assured McKinley: "The people of Cuba lend themselves readily to all sorts of demonstrations and parades, and little significance should be attached to them."

A committee was delegated by the Constitutional Convention to reply to the United States' insistence that the Platt Amendment e included in the Constitution. The committee report, "Penencia a la Convencion", was written by a black delegate from Santiago. It said:

"For the United States to reserve to itself the power to determine when this independence was threatened, and when, therefore, it should intervene to preserve it, is equivalent to handing over the keys to our house so that they can enter it at any time, whenever the desire seizes them, day or night, whether with good or evil design....

"The only Cuban governments that would live would be those which count on the support and benevolence of the United States, and the clearest result of this situation would be that we would only have feeble and miserable governments...condemned to live more attentive to obtaining the blessings of the United States than to serving and defending the interests f Cuba."

The report termed the provision for coaling or naval stations "a mutilation of the fatherland." It concluded:

"A people occupied militarily is being told that before consulting their own government, before being free in their own territory, they should grant the military occupants who came as friends and allies, rights and powers which would annul the sovereignty of these very people. That is the situation created for us by the method which the United States has just adopted. It could not be more obnoxious and inadmissible.

With this report, the Convention overwhelmingly rejected the Platt Amendment.

Within the next three months, however, the pressure from the United States, the military occupation, the refusal to allow the Cubans to set4 up their own government until they acquiesced, had its effect; the Convention, after several refusals, adopted the Platt Amendment. General Leonard Wood wrote in 190l to Theodore Roosevelt." There is, of course, little or no independence left Cuba under the Platt Amendment."

At this time, the United States was demanding an "open door" in China—to allow U.S. business interests to make China a sphere of influence.

But with the Monroe Doctrine, it had established a Closed Door in Latin America.

With the conquest of Cuba, the way was open for the United States to do as it wanted in the Caribbean. It soon engineered a revolution against Columbia and created the "independent' state of Panama in order to build and control the Canal across the Isthmus. In 1926 it would send five thousand marines to Nicaragua to forestall a revolution, keeping them there for seven years. The U.S. sent forces to occupy Haiti in 1915 and kept them there for nineteen years. It intervened in the Dominican Republic for the fourth time in 1916 and did not leave until 1924.

Between 1900 and 1933, the United States would send the marines to Cuba four times, to Nicaragua twice, to Panama six times, to Guatemala once, to Honduras seven times.

This is some of the historical background for U.S. policy towards Cuba in our time.

CHAPTER TWO

NOAM CHOMSKY

Described by the *New York Times* as "arguably the most important intellectual alive", Noam Chomsky is universally regarded as one of the most brilliant writers and thinkers. He is listed among the ten most cited writers in the humanities, and is the only living member of the top ten. An internationally acclaimed philosopher, scholar and political activist, he is Institute Professor in the Department of Linguistics and Philosophy at the Massachusetts Institute of Technology where he has taught since 1955.

Noam Chomsky's efforts for greater democracy are celebrated by peace and social movements worldwide.

He has published more than 70 books and thousands of articles on U.S. foreign policy, international affairs and the media. Among his numerous books are *The Culture of Terrorism*, *Profit over People*, *Deterring Democracy*, *Year 501*, *Propaganda and the Public Mind* and *Rogue States*.

His latest book is *Hegemony or Survival: America's Quest for Global Dominance*.

Cuba and the United States: A Near-Half Century of Terror

Cuba and the United States have quite a curious—in fact, unique—status in international relations. There is no similar case of such a sustained assault by one power against another—in this case the greatest superpower against a poor, Third World country—for more than 40 years of terror and economic warfare. The United States employed methods that ranged from a widespread campaign of terrorism to direct invasion. When the invasion failed, the terrorism campaign was intensified. This included economic strangulation, a cultural quarantine and the intimidation of anyone who attempted to break Cuba's isolation.

In fact, the fanaticism of this attack goes back a long, long time. From the first days of the American Revolution the eyes of the founding fathers were on Cuba. They were quite open about it. It was John Quincy Adams, when he was secretary of state, who said our taking Cuba is "of transcendent importance" to the political and commercial future of the United States. Others said that the future of the world depended on our taking Cuba. It was a matter "of transcendent importance" from the beginning of US history, and it remains so. The need to possess Cuba is the oldest issue in US foreign policy.

Cuba has brought real hysteria among planners. This was particularly striking during the Kennedy years. The internal records from the Kennedy administration, many of which are available now, describe an atmosphere of what was called "savagery" and "fanaticism" over the failure of the US to reconquer Cuba. Kennedy's own public statements were wild enough: "The complacent, the self-indulgent, the soft societies are about to be swept away with the debris of history," Kennedy railed outraged in this case by Cuba's unconscionable defeat of the Bay of Pigs invasion, unless it reincorporated Cuba under its control.

You will be pleased to know that the Pentagon recently downgraded the threat of Cuban conquest of the United States. It is still there, but it is not as serious as it was. The reason, they explained, is the deterioration of the awesome Cuban military forces after the end of the Cold War, when the Soviet Union stopped supplying them. So we can rest a little bit easier; we do not have to hide under tables the way we were taught to do in first grade. This elicited no ridicule when it was publicly announced, at least here. I am sure it did elsewhere; you might recall the response of the Mexican ambassador when John F. Kennedy was trying to organize collective security in defense against Cuba back in the early 60s in Mexico: the ambassador said he would regretfully have to decline because if he were to tell Mexicans that Cuba was a threat to their national security, 40 million Mexicans would die laughing.

The Batista dictatorship was overthrown in January 1959 by Castro's guerrilla forces. In March, the National Security Council (NSC) considered means to institute regime change. In May, the CIA began to arm guerrillas inside Cuba. "During the winter of 1959-1960, there was a significant increase in CIA-supervised bombing and incendiary raids piloted by exiled Cubans" based in the US. We need not tarry on what the US or its clients would do under such circumstances. Cuba, however, did not respond with violent actions within the United States for revenge or deterrence. Rather, it followed the procedure required by international law. In July 1960, Cuba called on the UN for help, providing the Security Council with records of some twenty bombings, including names of pilots, plane registration numbers, unexploded bombs, and other specific details, alleging considerable damage and casualties and calling for resolution of the conflict through diplomatic channels. US Ambassador Henry Cabot Lodge responded by giving his "assurance [that] the United States has no aggressive purpose against Cuba."

Cuba had been colonized by, and was entirely dependent on, the United States. Cuba was a virtual colony of the United States until January 1959; it did not take long before the wheels started turning again.

In March 1960 the Eisenhower administration secretly made a formal decision to conquer Cuba, but with a proviso: it had to be done in such a way that the US hand would not be evident. The reason for that was because they knew it would blow up Latin America if it were obvious that the US had retaken Cuba. Furthermore, they had polls indication that in Cuba itself there was a high level of optimism and strong support for the revolution;

there would obviously plenty of resistance. They had to overthrow he government, but in such a way that the US hand would not be evident. Accordingly, the ideological institutions must suppress the record of aggression, campaigns of terror, economic strangulation, and the other devices employed by the Lord of the hemisphere. They said their objective was to replace the Castro regime with one "more devoted to the true interests of the Cuban people and more acceptable to the US".

Washington was concerned that Cubans might try to defend themselves. CIA chief Allen Dulles therefore urged Britain not to provide arms to Cuba. His "main reason," the British ambassador reported to London, "was that this might lead the Cubans to ask for Soviet or Soviet bloc arms," a move that "would have a tremendous effect," Dulles pointed out, allowing Washington to portray Cuba as a security threat to the hemisphere, following the script that had worked so well in Guatemala. Dulles was referring to Washington's successful demolition of Guatemala's first democratic experiment, a ten-year interlude of hope and progress, greatly feared in Washington because of the enormous popular support reported by US intelligence and the "demonstration effect" of social and economic measures to benefit the large majority. The Soviet threat was routinely invoked, abetted by Guatemala's appeal to the Soviet bloc for arms after the US had threatened attack and cut off other sources of supply. The result was a half-century of horror, even worse than the US-backed tyranny that came before.

For Cuba, the schemes devised by the doves were similar to those of CIA director Dulles. Warning President Kennedy about the "inevitable political and diplomatic fall-out" from the planned invasion of Cuba by a proxy army, Arthur Schlesinger suggested efforts to trap Castro in some action that could be used as a pretext for invasion: "One can conceive a black operation in, say, Haiti which might in time lure Castro into sending a few boatloads of men on to a Haitian beach in what could be portrayed as an effort to overthrow the Haitian regime, then the moral issue would be clouded, and the anti-US campaign would be hobbled from the start." Reference is to the regime of the murderous dictator "Papa Doc" Duvalier, which was backed by the US (with some reservations), so that an effort to help Haitians overthrow it would be a crime.

The Kennedy administration came in. They were very much oriented towards Latin America; just before taking office Kennedy had established a Latin American mission to review the affairs of the continent. It was headed by historian Arthur Schlesinger. His report is now declassified. He informed President Kennedy of the results of the mission with regard to Cuba. The problem in Cuba, he said, is "the spread of the Castro idea that has a great deal of appeal throughout Latin America, where "the distribution of land and other forms of national wealth greatly favors the properties classes ... [and] the poor and underprivileged, stimulated by the example of the Cuban revolution, are now demanding opportunities for a decent living".[4] That is the threat of Castro. That is correct. In fact, if you read through the record of internal planning over the years, that has always been the threat. The Cold War is a public pretext. Take a look at the record; in case after case, it is exactly this. Cuba is what was called a "virus" that might infect others who might be stimulated by "the Castro idea of taking matters into [their] own hands" and believing that they too might have a decent living.

It is not that Russia was not mentioned. Russia is mentioned in the Schlesinger report. He says, in the background, Russia is offering itself as "the model for achieving modernization in a single generation," and is offering aid and development loans. So there was a Russian threat. We are instructed vigorously that when we inspect the new humanism, we are not supposed to look at those musty old stories about the Cold War, when we were blocked by the Russians from doing wonderful things. It is very important not to look, because the institutions have remained unchanged, the planning remains unchanged, the decisions are unchanged, and the policies are unchanged. It is far better to ensure that people do not know about them.

Sabotage, terror, and aggression were escalated further by the Kennedy administration, along with the kind of economic warfare that no small country can endure. Cuban reliance on the US as an export market and for imports had, of course, been overwhelming, and could hardly be replaced without cost. The New Frontiersmen were obsessed with Cuba the first moments. During the presidential campaign of 1960, Kennedy had accused Eisenhower and Nixon of threatening US security by allowing "the Iron Curtain…90 miles off the cost of the United States." "We were hysterical about Castro at the time of the Bay of Pigs [April 1961] and thereafter," Defense Secretary Robert McNamara later testified to the Church Committee. A few days before the decision to invade Cuba, Arthur Schlesinger advised the President that "the game would be up through a good deal of Latin America" if the US were to tolerate "another Cuba"; or this one, JFK determined. Much of Kennedy's Latin American policy was inspired by the fear that the virus would infect others and limit US hegemony.[5]

Immediately after the Bay of Pigs failure, Kennedy initiated a program of international terrorism to overthrow the regime, reaching quite remarkable dimensions. These atrocities are largely dismissed in the West, apart from some notice of the assassination attempts, one of them implemented on the very day of the Kennedy assassination. The terrorist operations were formally called off by Lyndon Johnson. They continued, however, and were escalated by Nixon. Subsequent actions are attributed to renegades beyond CIA control, whether accurately or not, we do no know; one high-level Pentagon official of the Kennedy-Johnson Administrations, Roswell Gilpatric, has expressed his doubts. The Carter

Administration, with the support of US courts, condoned hijacking of Cuban ships in violation of the anti-hijacking convention that Castro was respecting. The Reaganites rejected Cuban initiatives Cuban initiatives for diplomatic settlement and imposed new sanctions on the most outlandish pretexts, often lying outright, a record reviewed by Wayne Smith, who resigned as head of the US Interests Section in Havana in protest.[6]

From the Cuban perspective, the Kennedy terror seemed to be a prelude to invasion. The CIA concluded in September 1962—before the Russian missiles were detected in mid-October—that " the main purpose of the present [Soviet] military buildup in Cuba is to strengthen the Communist regime there against what the Cubans and Soviets conceive to be a danger that the US may attempt by one means or another to overthrow it." In early October, the State Department confirmed this judgment, as did a later State Department confirmed this judgment, as did a later State Department study.

Of interest, in this connection, is Robert McNamara's reaction to the late Andrei Gromyko's allegation that missiles were sent to Cuba "to strengthen the defensive capability of Cuba—that is all." In response McNamara acknowledged that "If I had been a Cuban or Soviet official, I believe I would have shared the judgment you expressed that a U.S. invasion was probable" (a judgment that he says was inaccurate). The probability of nuclear war after a US invasion was "99 percent," McNamara added. Such an invasion was frighteningly close after JFK dismissed Khrushchev's offer of mutual withdrawal of missiles from Cuba and Turkey (the latter obsolete, already ordered withdrawn). Indeed, Cuba itself might have initiated nuclear war when a US terrorist (Mongoose) team blew up a factory, killing 400 people according to Castro, at one of the most tense moments of the crisis, when the Cubans may have had their fingers on the button.[7]

Matters continued up until the end of the Cold War and the

US pursued its venerable task of preventing Cuban independence, with 170 years of experience behind it. It is not that nothing changed at the end of the Cold War; it did. The main thing that changed was that there no longer was a Soviet deterrent. No longer was Cuba an agent of the Kremlin, bent on taking over Latin America and conquering the United States, trembling in terror. That meant that the US was much more free than before, along with its loyal attack dog, the UK. So the US and UK are now much more free to use force than they were when there was a deterrent. That was recognized right away. But new pretexts are needed. You can no longer say that everything we do is against the Russians.

With regard to Cuba, right after the fall of the Soviet Union in 1991, the embargo became far harsher, under a liberal initiative, incidentally: it was a Torricelli-Clinton initiative. And the pretexts were now different. Before, it was that the Cubans were a tentacle of the Soviet beast about to strangle us; now it was suddenly our love of democracy that made us oppose Cuba. The lies of 30 years can be quietly shelved: terror and economic warfare have always been an attempt to bring democracy, in the revised standard version.

The US does support a certain kind of democracy. The kind of democracy it supports was described rather frankly by a leading scholar who dealt with the democratic initiatives of the Reagan administration in the 1980s and who writes from an insider's point of view because he was in the State Department working on "democracy enhancement" projects: Thomas Carothers. He points out that though the Reagan administration, which he thinks was very sincere, undermined democracy everywhere, it nevertheless was interested in a certain kind of democracy—what he calls "top-down" forms of democracy that leave "traditional structures of power" in place, namely those with which the US has long had good relations. As long as democracy has that form, it is no a problem.

***

The US sanctions against Cuba are the harshest in the world, much harsher than the sanctions against Iraq were, for example. They have been in force since 1960, but became much more severe, with a heavy human toll, when the "monolithic and ruthless conspiracy" finally faded away and it was impossible any longer to appeal to the grave national security threat posed by Cuba—far short of the threat posed by Denmark or Luxembourg to the USSR. These unilateral coercive measures do not count as a "sanctions regime", however. They are "strictly a matter of bilateral trade policy and not a matter appropriate for consideration by the UN General Assembly", so the US explained in response to the UN vote (Deputy US Representative to the UN Peter Burleigh, speaking to the General Assembly, reiterated by the State Department). Repeating almost verbatim Washington's reaction to the seven previous years' votes, Philip Reeker, a State Department spokesman, said that "the trade embargo is US law which we will enforce". It makes no difference what the world might think or decide.

There was a small item in the *New York Times* recently that said that Congress is passing legislation to allow US exporters to send food and medicine to Cuba. It explained that this was the urging of US farmers. "Farmers" is a euphemism that means "US agribusiness"—it sounds better when you call them "farmers". And it is true that US agribusiness wants to get back into this market. The article did not point out that the restriction against the sale and export of food and medicines is in gross violation of international humanitarian law. It has been condemned by almost every relevant body. Even the normally quite compliant Organization of American States, which rarely stands up against the boss, did condemn this as illegal and unacceptable.

US policy towards Cuba is unique in a variety of respects,

first of all because of the sustained attacks, and secondly because the US is totally isolated in the world—in fact, 100 percent isolated, because the one state that reflexively has to vote with the United States at the UN, Israel, also openly violates the embargo, contrary to its vote.

The United States government is also isolated from its own population. According to the most recent poll I have seen, about two-thirds of the population of the United States is opposed to the embargo. They do not take polls in the business world, but there is pretty strong evidence that major sectors of the business world, major corporations, are strongly opposed to the embargo. So the isolation of the US government is another unusual element. The US government is isolated from its own population, from the major decision makers in this society, which largely control the government, and from international opinion, but is fanatically committed to this policy, which goes right back to the roots of the American republic.

Clinton's "Cuban Democracy Act"—which President Bush at first vetoed because it was so transparently in violation of international law, and then signed when he was outflanked from the right by Clinton during the election campaign—cut off trade by US subsidiaries abroad, 90 per cent of it food, medicine and medical equipment. That contribution to democracy helped to bring about a considerable decline in Cuban health standards, an increase in mortality rates, and "the most alarming public health crisis in Cuba in recent memory", according to the former chief camps of neuro-epidemiology at the National Institute of Health. To illustrate the effects, a Columbia University Professor of Medicine cites the case of a Swedish water filtration system that Cuba had purchased to produce vaccines, barred because some parts are produced by an American-owned company, so life-saving vaccines can be denied to bring "democracy" to the survivors.

In 1997 at the World Trade Organization (WTO) when the

European Union brought charges against the United States for blatant, flagrant violation of WTO rules in the embargo, the US rejected its jurisdiction, which is not surprising, because it rejects the jurisdiction of international bodies generally. But the reasons were interesting. It rejected its jurisdiction on the grounds of a national security reservation. The national security of the United States was threatened by the existence of Cuba, and therefore the US had to reject WTO jurisdiction. Actually, the US did not make that position official, because it would have subjected itself to international ridicule, but that was the position, and it was publicly stated, repeatedly. It is a national security issue; we therefore cannot consider WTO jurisdiction.

***

The real problem of Cuba remains what it has always been. It remains the threat of "the Castro idea of taking matters into [your] own hands," which continues to be a stimulus to poor and underprivileged people who cannot get it driven into their heads that they have no right to seek opportunities for a decent living. And Cuba, unfortunately, keeps making that clear, for example, by sending doctors all over the world at a rate way beyond any other country despite its current straits, which are severe, and by maintaining, unimaginably, a health system that is a deep embarrassment to the United States. Because of concerns such as these, and because of the fanaticism that goes way back in American history, the US government, for the moment, at least, is continuing the hysterical attack, and will do so until it is deterred.

The terrorist campaign was "no laughing matter," Jorge Dominguez writes in a review of recently declassified materials on operations under Kennedy, materials that are "heavily sanitized" and "only the tip of the iceberg," Piero Gleijeses adds.

Operation Mongoose was "the centerpiece of American policy

toward Cuba from late 1961 until the onset of the 1962 missile crisis," Mark White reports, the program on which the Kennedy brothers "came to pin their hopes." Robert Kennedy informed the CIA that the Cuban problem carries "the top priority in the United States Government—all else is secondary—no time, no effort, or manpower is to be spared" in the effort to overthrow the Castro regime. The chief of Mongoose operations, Edward Lansdale, provided a timetable leading to "open revolt and overthrow of the Communist regime" in October 1962. The "final definition" of the program recognized that "final success will require decisive U.S. military intervention," after terrorism and subversion had laid the basis. The implication is that US military intervention would take place in October 1962—when the missile crisis erupted.

In February 1962, the Joint Chiefs of Staff approved a plan more extreme than Schlesinger's: to use "covert means to lure or provoke Castro, or an uncontrollable subordinate, into an overt hostile reaction against the United States; a reaction which would in turn create the justification for the US to not only retaliate but destroy Castro with speed, force and determination." In March, at the request of the DOD Cuba Project, the Joint Chiefs of Staff submitted a memorandum to Defense Secretary Robert McNamara outlining "pretexts which they would consider would provide justification for US military intervention in Cuba." The plan would be undertaken if "a credible internal revolt is impossible of attainment during the next 9-10 months," but before Cuba could establish relations with Russia that might "directly involve the Soviet Union."

The March plan was to construct "seemingly unrelated events to camouflage the ultimate objective and create the necessary impression of Cuban rashness and responsibility on a large scale, directed at other countries as well as the United States," placing the US "in the apparent position of suffering defensible grievances [and developing] an international image of Cuban threat to peace in the Western Hemisphere." Proposed measures included blowing up a US ship in Guantanamo Bay to create "a 'Remember the *Maine*' incident," publishing casualty lists in US newspapers to "cause a helpful wave of national indignation," portraying Cuban investigations as "fairly compelling evidence that the ship was taken under attack," developing a "Communist Cuban terror campaign [in Florida] and even in Washington," using Soviet bloc incendiaries for cane-burning raids in neighboring countries, shooting down a drone aircraft with a pretense that it was a charter flight carrying college students on a holiday, and other similarly ingenious schemes—not implemented, but another sign of the "frantic" and "savage" atmosphere that prevailed.

On August 23 the president issued National Security Memorandum No. 181, "a directive to engineer an internal revolt that would be followed by U.S. military intervention," involving "significant U.S. military plans, maneuvers, and movement of forces and equipment" that were surely known to Cuba and Russia. Also in August, terrorist attacks were intensified, including speedboat strafing attacks on a Cuban seaside hotel "where Soviet military technicians were known to congregate, killing a score of Russians and Cubans"; attacks on British and Cuban cargo ships; the contamination of sugar shipments; and other atrocities and sabotage, mostly carried out by Cuban exile organizations permitted to operate freely in Florida. A few weeks later came "the most dangerous moment in human history."

After the missiles crisis ended, Kennedy renewed the terrorist campaign. Ten days before his assassination he approved a CIA plan for "destruction operations" by US proxy forces "against a large oil refinery and storage facilities, a large electric plant, sugar refineries, railroad bridges, harbor facilities, and underwater demolition of docks and ships." A plot to kill Castro was initiated on the day of the Kennedy assassination. The campaign was called off in 1965, but "one of Nixon's first acts in office in 1969 was to direct the CIA to intensify covert operations against Cuba."

Of particular interest are the perceptions of the planners. In his review of recently released documents on Kennedy-era terror, Dominguez observes that "only once in these nearly thousand pages of documentation did a U.S. official raise something that resembled a faint moral objection to U.S.-government sponsored terrorism": a member of the NSC staff suggested that it might lead to some Russian reaction, and raids that are "haphazard and kill innocents might mean a bad press in some friendly countries." The same attitudes prevail throughout the internal discussions, as when Robert Kennedy warned that a full-scale invasion of Cuba would "kill an awful lot of people, and we're going to take an awful lot of heat on it."

Terrorist activities continued under Nixon, peaking in the mid—1970s, with attacks on fishing boats, embassies, and Cuban offices overseas, and the bombing of a Cubana airliner, killing all seventy-three passengers. These and subsequent terrorist operations were carried out from US territory, though by then they were regarded as criminal acts by the FBI.

So matters proceeded, while Castro was condemned by editors for maintaining an "armed camp, despite the security from attack promised by Washington in 1962." The promise should have sufficed, despite what followed; not to speak of the promises that preceded, by then well documented, along with information about how well they could be trusted: e.g., the "Lodge moment" of July 1960.

The reasons for the international terrorist attacks against Cuba and the illegal economic embargo are spelled out in the internal record. And no one should be surprised to discover that they fit a familiar pattern—that of Guatemala a few years earlier, for example.

From the timing alone, it is clear that concern over a Russian threat could not have been a major factor. The plans for forceful regime change were drawn up and implemented before there was any significant Russian connection, and punishment was intensified after the Russians disappeared from the scene. True, a Russian threat did develop, but that was more a consequence than a cause of US terrorism and economic warfare.

In July 1961 the CIA warned that "the extensive influence of 'Castroism' is not a function of Cuban power. Castro's shadow looms large because social and economic conditions throughout Latin America invite opposition to ruling authority and encourage agitation for radical change," for which Castro's Cuba provided a model.

In early 1964, the State Department Policy Planning Council expanded on these concerns: "The primary danger we face in Castro is...in the impact the very existence of his regime has upon the leftist movement in many Latin American countries.... The simple fact is that Castro represents a successful defiance of the US, a negation of our whole hemispheric policy of almost a century and a half." To put it simply, Thomas Paterson writes, "Cuba, as symbol and reality, challenged U.S. hegemony in Latin America." International terrorism and economic warfare to bring about regime change are justified not by what Cuba does, but by its "very existence," its "successful defiance" of the proper master of the hemisphere. Defiance may justify even more violent actions, as in Serbia, as quietly conceded after the fact; or Iraq, as also recognized when pretexts had collapsed.

***

On the thirtieth anniversary of the missile crisis, Cuba protested a machine-gun attack against a Spanish-Cuban tourist hotel; responsibility was claimed by a group in Miami. Bombings in Cuba in 1997, which killed an Italian tourist, were traced back to Miami. The perpetrators were Salvadoran criminals operating under the direction of Luis Posada Carriles and financed in Miami. One of the most notorious international terrorists, Posada had escaped from a Venezuelan prison, where he had been held for the Cubana airliner bombing, with the aid of Jorge Mas Canosa, a Miami businessman who was the head of the tax-exempt Cuban-American National Foundation (CANF). Posada went from Venezuela to El Salvador, where he was put to work at the Ilopango military air base to help organize US terrorist attacks against Nicaragua under Oliver North's direction.

Posada has described in detail his terrorist activities and the funding for them from exiles and CANF in Miami, but felt secure that he would not be investigated by the FBI. He was a Bay of Pigs veteran, and his subsequent operations in the 1960s were directed by the CIA. When he later joined Venezuelan intelligence with CIA help, he was able to arrange for Orlando Bosch, an associate from his CIA days who had been convicted in the US for a bomb attack on a Cuba-bound freighter, to join him in Venezuela to organize further attacks against Cuba. An ex-CIA official familiar with the Cubana bombing identifies Posada and Bosch as the only suspects in the bombing, which Bosch defended as "a legitimate act of war." Generally considered the "mastermind" of the airline bombing, Bosch was responsible for thirty other acts of terrorism, according to the FBI. He was granted a presidential pardon in 1989 by the incoming Bush I administration after intense lobbying by Jeb Bush and South Florida Cuban-American leaders, overruling the Justice Department, which had found the conclusion "inescapable that it would be prejudicial to the public interest for the United States to provide a safe haven for Bosch [because] the security of this nation is affected by its ability to urge credibly other nations to refuse aid and shelter to terrorists."

Cuban offers to cooperate in intelligence-sharing to prevent terrorist attacks have been rejected by Washington, though some did lead to US actions. "Senior members of the FBI visited Cuba in 1998 to meet their Cuban counterparts, who gave [the FBI] dossiers about what they suggested was a Miami-based terrorist network: information which had been compiled in part by Cubans who had infiltrated exile groups." Three months later the FBI arrested Cubans who had infiltrated the US-based terrorist groups. Five were sentenced to long terms in prison.

In respected scholarship, US terrorism against Cuba has been excised from the record in a display of servility that would impress the most dedicated totalitarian. In the media, Cuba's plight is regularly attributed to the demon Castro and "Cuban socialism" alone. Castro bears full responsibility for the "poverty, isolation and humbling dependence" on the USSR, the *New York Times* editors inform us, concluding triumphantly that the "Cuba dictator has painted himself into his own corner", without any help from us. That is true by virtue of doctrinal necessity, the ultimate authority. The editors conclude that we should not intervene directly as some "U.S. cold warriors" propose: "Fidel Castro's reign deserves to end in home-grown failure, not martyrdom." Taking their stand at the dovish extreme, the editors advise that we should continue to stand aside, watching in silence as we have been doing for 30 years, so the naïve reader would learn from this (quite typical) version of history, crafted to satisfy the demands of authority.

The Cuban record demonstrates with great clarity that the Cold War framework has been scarcely more than a pretext to conceal the standard refusal to tolerate Third World independence, whatever its political coloration. Traditional policies remain beyond serious challenge within the mainstream. The most obvious questions are ruled illegitimate, if not unthinkable.

CHAPTER THREE

WILLIAM BLUM

William Blum left the State Department in 1967, abandoning his aspiration of becoming a Foreign Service Officer, because of his opposition to what the United States was doing in Vietnam. He then became on of the founders and editors of the Washington Free Press, the first "alternative" newspaper in the capital.

In 1969, he wrote and published an exposé of the CIA in which was revealed the names and addresses of more than 200 employees of the Agency. In the Mid-1970's, he worked in London with former CIA officer Philip Agee and his associates on their project of exposing CIA personnel and their misdeeds.

The late 1980s found Mr. Blum living in Los Angeles, teaching and pursuing a career as a screenwriter. Unfortunately, his screenplays all had two (if not three) strikes against them because they dealt with those things which makes grown men run screaming in Hollywood: Ideas and issues.

Currently, he is living in Washington, DC again, making use of the Library of Congress and the National Archives, and striking fear into the hearts of US government imperialists.

His book *Killing Hope: U.S. Military and CIA Interventions since World War II* is a valuable reference indispensable to understand U.S. foreign policy.

The Unforgivable Revolution

In the American lexicon, in addition to good and bad bases and missiles, there are good and bad revolutions. The American and French Revolutions were good. The Cuban Revolution is bad.

After the Cuban Revolution in January 1959, we learned that there are also good and bad hijackings. On several occasions Cuban planes and boats were hijacked to the United States but they were not returned to Cuba, nor were the hijackers punished. Instead, some of the planes and boats were seized by US authorities for non-payment of debts claimed by American firms against the Cuban government.[1] But then there were the bad hijackings—planes forced to fly from the United States to Cuba. When there began to be more of these than flights in the opposite direction, Washington was obliged to reconsider its policy.

It appears that there are as well good and bad terrorists. When the Israelis bombed LO headquarters in Tunis in 1985, Ronald Reagan expressed his approval. The president asserted that nations have the right to retaliate against terrorist attacks "as long as you pick out the people responsible".[2]

But if Cuba had dropped bombs on any of the headquarters of the anti-Castro exiles in Miami or New Jersey, Ronald Reagan would likely have gone to war, though for 25 years the Castro government had been on the receiving end of an extraordinary series of terrorist attacks carried out in Cuba, in the United States, and in other countries by the exiles and their CIA mentors. (We shall not discuss the consequences of Cuba bombing CIA headquarters.)

Bombing and strafing attacks of Cuba by planes based in the United States began in October 1959, if not before.[3] In early 1960, there were several fire-bomb air raids on Cuban cane fields and sugar mills, in which American pilots also took part—at least three of whom died in crashes, while two others were captured. The State Department acknowledged that one plane which crashed, killing two Americans, had taken off from Florida, but insisted that it was against the wishes of the US government.[4]

In March a French freighter unloading munitions from Belgium exploded in Havana taking 75 lives and injuring 200, some of whom subsequently died. The United States denied Cuba's accusation of sabotage but admitted that it had sought to prevent the shipment.[5]

And so it went...reaching a high point in April of the following year in the infamous CIA-organized invasion of Cuba at the Bay of Pigs. Over 100 exiles died in the attack. Close to 1,200 others were taken prisoner by the Cubans. It was later revealed that four American pilots flying for the CIA had lost their lives as well.[6]

The Bay of Pigs assault had relied heavily on the Cuban people rising up to join the invaders,[7] but this was not to be the case. As it was, the leadership and ranks of the exile forces were riddled with former supporters and henchmen of Fulgencio Batista, the dictator overthrown by Castro, and would not have been welcomed back by the Cuban people under any circumstances.

Despite the fact that the Kennedy administration was acutely embarrassed by the unmitigated defeat—indeed, *because* of it—a campaign of smaller-scale attacks upon Cuba was initiated almost immediately, under the rubric of Operation Mongoose. Throughout the 1960s, the Caribbean island was subjected to countless sea and air commando raids by exiles, at times accompanied by their CIA supervisors, inflicting damage upon oil refineries, chemical plants and railroad bridges, cane fields, sugar mills and sugar warehouses; infiltrating spies, saboteurs and assassins...anything to damage the Cuban economy, promote disaffection, or make the revolution look bad...taking the lives of Cuban militia members and others in the process... pirate attacks on Cuban fishing boats and merchant ships, bombardments of Soviet vessels docked in Cuba, an assault upon a Soviet army camp with 12 Russian soldiers reported wounded...a hotel and a theatre shelled from offshore because Russians and East Europeans were supposed to be present there.[8]

These actions were not always carried out on the direct order of the CIA or with its foreknowledge, but the Agency could hardly plead "rogue elephant". It had created Operation Mongoose headquarters in Miami that was truly a state within a city—over, above, and outside the laws of the United States, not to mention international law, with a staff of several hundred Americans directing many more Cuban agents in just such types of actions, with a budget in excess of $50 million a year, and an arrangement with the local press to keep operations in Florida secret except when the CIA wanted something publicized.[9]

Title 18 of the US Code declares it to be a crime to launch a "military or naval expedition or enterprise" from the United States against a country with which the United States is not (officially) at war. Although US authorities now and then aborted an exile plot or impounded a boat—sometimes because the Coast Guard or other officials had not been properly clued in—no Cubans were prosecuted under this act. This was no more than to be expected inasmuch as Attorney General Robert Kennedy had determined after the Bay of Pigs that the invasion did not constitute a military expedition.[10]

The commando raids were combined with a total US trade and credit embargo, which continues to this day, and which genuinely hurt the Cuban economy and chipped away at the society's standard of living. So unyielding has the embargo been that when Cuba was hard hit by a hurricane in October 1963, and Casa Cuba, a New York social club, raised a large quantity of clothing for relief, the United States refused to grant it an export license on the grounds that such shipment was "contrary to the national interest".[11]

What undoubtedly was an even more sensitive venture was the use of chemical and biological weapons against Cuba by the United States. It is a remarkable record.

In August 1962, a British freighter under Soviet lease, having damaged its propeller on a reef, crept into the harbor at San Juan, Puerto Rico for repairs. It was bound for a Soviet port with

80,000 bags of Cuban sugar. The ship was put into dry dock and 14,135 sacks of sugar were unloaded to a warehouse to facilitate the repairs. While in the warehouse, the sugar was contaminated by CIA agents with a substance that was allegedly harmless but unpalatable. When President Kennedy learned of the operation he was furious because it had taken place in US territory and if discovered could provide the Soviet Union with a propaganda field day and could set a terrible precedent for chemical sabotage in the cold war. He directed that the sugar not be returned to the Russians, although what explanation was given to them is not publicly known.[12] Similar undertakings were apparently not canceled. The CIA official who helped direct worldwide sabotage efforts, referred to above, later revealed that "There was lots of sugar being sent out from Cuba, and we were putting a lot of contaminants in it."[13]

The same year, a Canadian agricultural technician working as an adviser to the Cuban government was paid $5,000 by "an American military intelligence agent" to infect Cuban turkeys with a virus which would produce the fatal Newcastle disease. Subsequently, 8,000 turkeys died. The technician later claimed that although he had been to the farm where the turkeys had died, he had not actually administered the virus, but had instead pocketed the money, and that the turkeys had died from neglect and other causes unrelated to the virus. This may have been a self-serving statement. The *Washington Post* reported that "According to U.S. intelligence reports, the Cubans—and some Americans—believe the turkeys died as the result of espionage."[14]

Authors Warren Hinckle and William Turner, citing a participant in the project, have reported in their book on Cuba that:

During 1969 and 1970, the CIA deployed futuristic weather modification technology to ravage Cuba's sugar crop and undermine the economy. Planes from the China Lake Naval Weapons Center in the California desert, where hi tech was developed, overflew the island, seeding rain clouds with crystals that precipitated torrential rains over non-agricultural areas and left the cane fields arid (the downpours caused killer flash floods in some areas).[15]

In 1971, also according to participants, the CIA turned over to Cuban exiles a virus which causes African swine fever. Six weeks later, an outbreak of the disease in Cuba forced the slaughter of 500,000 pigs to prevent a nationwide animal epidemic. The outbreak, the first ever in the Western hemisphere, was called the "most alarming event" of the year by the United Nations Food and Agricultural Organization.[16]

Ten years later, the target may well have been human beings, as an epidemic of dengue fever swept the Cuban island. Transmitted by blood-eating insects, usually mosquitos, the disease produces severe flu symptoms and incapacitating bone pain. Between May and October 1981, over 300,000 cases were reported in Cuba with 158 fatalities, 101 of which were children under 15.[17] In 1956 and 1958, declassified documents have revealed, the US Army loosed swarms of specially bred mosquitos in Georgia and Florida to see whether disease-carrying insects could be weapons in a biological war. The mosquitos bred for the tests were of the Aedes Aegypti type, the precise carrier of dengue fever as well as other diseases.[18] In 1967 it was reported by Science magazine that at the US government center in Fort Detrick, Maryland, dengue fever was amongst those "diseases that are at least the objects of considerable research and that appear to be among those regarded as potential BW [biological warfare] agents."[19] Then, in 1984, a Cuban exile on trial in New York testified that in the latter part of 1980 a ship traveled from Florida to Cuba with a mission to carry some germs to introduce them in Cuba to be used against the Soviets and against the Cuban economy, to begin what was called chemical war, which later on produced results that were not what we had expected, because we thought that it was going to be used against the Soviet forces, and it was used against our own people, and with that we did not agree.[20]

It's not clear from the testimony whether the Cuban man thought that the germs would somehow be able to confine their actions to only Russians, or whether he had been misled by the people behind the operation.

The full extent of American chemical and biological warfare against Cuba will never be known. Over the years, the Castro government has in fact blamed the United States for a number of other plagues which afflicted various animals and crops.[21] And in 1977, newly-released CIA documents disclosed that the Agency "maintained a clandestine anti-crop warfare research program targeted during the 1960s at a number of countries throughout the world."[22]

It came to pass that the United States felt the need to put some of its chemical and biological warfare (CBW) expertise into the hands of other nations. As of 1969, some 550 students, from 36 countries, had completed courses at the US Army's Chemical School at Fort McClellan, Alabama. The CBW instruction was provided to the students under the guise of "defense" against such weapons—just as in Vietnam, as we have seen, torture was taught. As will be described in the chapter on Uruguay, the manufacture and use of bombs was taught under the cover of combating terrorist bombings.[23]

The ingenuity which went into the chemical and biological warfare against Cuba was apparent in some of the dozens of plans to assassinate or humiliate Fidel Castro. Devised by the CIA or Cuban exiles, with the cooperation of American mafiosi, the plans ranged from poisoning Castro's cigars and food to a chemical designed to make his hair and beard fall off and LSD to be administered just before a public speech. There were also of course the more traditional approaches of gun and bomb, one being an attempt to drop bombs on a baseball stadium while Castro was speaking; the

B-26 bomber was driven away by anti-aircraft fire before it could reach the stadium.[24] It is a combination of such Cuban security measures, informers, incompetence, and luck which has served to keep the bearded one alive to the present day.

Attempts were also made on the lives of Castro's brother Raul and Che Guevara. The latter was the target of a bazooka fired at the United Nations building in New York in December 1964.[25] Various Cuban exile groups have engaged in violence on a regular basis in the United States with relative impunity for decades. One of them, going by the name of Omega 7 and headquartered in Union City, New Jersey, was characterized by the FBI in 1980 as "the most dangerous terrorist organization in the United States".[26] Attacks against Cuba itself began to lessen around the end of the 1960s, due probably to a lack of satisfying results combined with ageing warriors, and exile groups turned to targets in the United States and elsewhere in the world.

During the next decade, while the CIA continued to pour money into the exile community, more than 100 serious "incidents" took place in the United States for which Omega 7 and other groups claimed responsibility. (Within the community, the distinction between a terrorist and a non-terrorist group is not especially precise; there is much overlapping identity and frequent creation of new names.) There occurred repeated bombings of the Soviet UN Mission, its Washington embassy, its automobiles, a Soviet ship docked in New Jersey, the offices of the Soviet airline Aeroflot, with a number of American policemen and Russians injured in these attacks; several bombings of the Cuban UN Mission and its Interests Section in Washington, many attacks upon Cuban diplomats, including at least one murder; a bomb discovered at New York's Academy of Music in 1976 shortly before a celebration of the Cuban Revolution was to begin; a bombing two years later of the Lincoln Center after the Cuban ballet had performed; three bombings in a single night in 1979:

the office of a New Jersey Cuban refugee program, a New Jersey pharmacy that sent medical supplies to Cuba, and a suitcase that exploded at JFK Airport, injuring four luggage handlers, minutes before it was to be placed aboard a TWA flight to Los Angeles.[27]

The single most violent act of this period was the blowing up of a Cubana Airlines plane shortly after it took off from Barbados on 6 October 1976, which took the lives of 73 people including the entire Cuban championship fencing team. CIA documents later revealed that on 22 June, a CIA officer abroad had cabled a report to Agency headquarters that he had learned from a source that a Cuban exile group planned to bomb a Cubana airliner flying between Panama and Havana. The group's leader was a baby doctor named Orlando Bosch. After the plane crashed in the sea in October, it was Bosch's network of exiles that claimed responsibility. The cable showed that the CIA had the means to penetrate the Bosch organization, but there's no indication in any of the documents that the Agency undertook any special monitoring of Bosch and his group because of their plans, or that the CIA warned Havana.[28]

In 1983, while Orlando Bosch sat in a Venezuelan prison charged with masterminding the plane bombing, the City Commission of Miami proclaimed a "Dr. Orlando Bosch Day".[29] In 1968, Bosch had been convicted of a bazooka attack on a Polish ship in Miami.

Cuban exiles themselves have often come in for harsh treatment. Those who have visited Cuba for any reason whatever, or publicly suggested, however timidly, a rapprochement with the homeland, they too have been the victims of bombings and shootings in Florida and New Jersey. American groups advocating a resumption of diplomatic relations or an end to the embargo have been similarly attacked, as have travel agencies handling trips to Cuba and a pharmaceutical company in New Jersey which shipped medicines to the island.

Dissent in Miami has been effectively silenced, while the police, city officials, and the media look the other way, when not actually demonstrating support for the exiles' campaign of intimidation.[30] In Miami and elsewhere, the CIA—ostensibly to uncover Castro agents—has employed exiles to spy on their countrymen, to keep files on them, as well as on Americans who associate with them.[31]

Although there has always been the extreme lunatic fringe in the Cuban exile community (as opposed to the normal lunatic fringe) insisting that Washington has sold out their cause, over the years there has been only the occasional arrest and conviction of an exile for a terrorist attack in the United States, so occasional that the exiles can only assume that Washington's heart is not wholly in it. The exile groups and their key members are well known to the authorities, for the anti-Castroites have not excessively shied away from publicity. At least as late as the early 1980s, they were training openly in southern Florida and southern California; pictures of them flaunting their weapons appeared in the press.[32] The CIA, with its countless contacts-cum-informers amongst the exiles, could fill in many of the missing pieces for the FBI and the police, if it wished to. In 1980, in a detailed report on Cuban-exile terrorism, The Village Voice of New York reported:

Two stories were squeezed out of New York police officials..."You know, it's funny," said one cautiously, "there have been one or two things...but let's put it this way. You get just so far on a case and suddenly the dust is blown away. Case closed. You ask the CIA to help, and they say they aren't really interested. You get the message." Another investigator said he was working on a narcotics case involving Cuban exiles a couple of years ago, and telephone records he obtained showed a frequently dialed number in Miami. He said he traced the number to a company called Zodiac, "which turned out to be a CIA front." He dropped his investigation.[33]

The Cuban exiles in the United States, collectively, may well constitute the longest lasting and most prolific terrorist group in the world. It is thus the height of irony, not to mention hypocrisy, that for many years up to the present time, the State Department has included Cuba amongst those nations that "sponsor terrorism", not because of any terrorist acts committed by the Cuban government, but solely because they "harbor terrorists".

Haven for Terrorists

In 1998, the State Department issued its annual human rights report, listing Cuba amongst those nations alleged to "sponsor terrorism". Curious about this, I called up the State Department and was connected to what they called "The Terrorism Desk", where a gentleman named Joe Reap told me that Cuba was included because "They harbor terrorists."

"So does the United States," I replied. "The Cuban exiles in Miami have committed hundreds of terrorist acts, in the US an abroad."

Mr. Reap exploded. "Sir," he cried in a rising voice, "that is a fatuous remark and I will not listen to such nonsense!" And he hung up.

Unrepentant trouble-maker that I am, the following year, May 4, 1999 to be exact, when the new human-rights report was issued (does the word "self-righteous" ring a bell with the folks at the State Department?), I again called 202-647-8682, and again 'twas Joe Reap who answered. I doubt he knew that I was the same caller as the year before but, in any event, we went through the same dance steps. When I repeated my comment about the Cuban terrorists being harbored in Miami, he became instantly indignant and said that they were not terrorists.

"But the FBI had labeled some of them just that," I said.

"Then take it up with the FBI," said Joe.

"But we are discussing a State Department report," I pointed out.

His voice rising... "I will not listen to people call this government a terrorist sponsor!" Phone slammed down. The intervening year had not mellowed ol' Joe any more than it had me.

It is always fascinating to observe how a true Believer reacts to a sudden, unexpected and unanswerable threat to his fundamental ideological underpinnings.

The Cuban exiles are in fact one of the longest lasting and most prolific terrorist groups in the world, and they are still at it. During 1997 they carried out a spate of bombings in Havana, directed from Miami.[34]

Hijacking is generally regarded as a grave international crime, but although there have been some numerous air and boat hijacking over the years from Cuba to the US, at gunpoint, knifepoint and/or with the use of physical force, including at least one murder, it is difficult to find more than a single instance where the United States brought criminal charges against the hijackers. In August 1996, three Cubans who hijacked a plane to Florida at knifepoint were indicted and brought to trial. In Florida. This is like trying someone for gambling in a Nevada court. Even though the kidnapped pilot was brought back from Cuba to testify against the men, the defense simply told the jurors that the man was lying, and the jury deliberated less than an hour before acquitting the defendants.[35]

Presidential Decision Directive 39, signed by President Clinton in 1995, states:

If we do not receive adequate cooperation from a state that harbors a terrorist whose extradition we are seeking, we shall take appropriate measures to induce cooperation. Return of suspects by force may be affected without the cooperation of the host government.[36]

So determined was the Clinton administration to punish other states that compete with the US in harboring terrorists, that in February 1999 it asserted the right to bomb government facilities in such nations. "We may not just go in a strike against a terrorist facility; we may choose to retaliate against the facilities of the host country, if that host country is a knowing, cooperative sanctuary," Richard Clarke, President Clinton's coordinator for counter-terrorism, declared.[37]

I tried to reach Mr. Clarke at his White House office to ask him what he thought of the proposition that Cuba could justifiably designate the United States as a "knowing, cooperative sanctuary" and bomb CIA headquarters or a Cuban exile office in Miami, amongst other sites. However, I was told that he was "not available to the general public to speak to". Pity. So I sent him a letter posing these questions, with little expectation of an answer. I was not disappointed.

Cuban Political Prisoners...in the United States

The Florida Association of Criminal Defense Lawyers gave the defense team its "Against All Odds" award, established in honor of a deceased public defender who championed hopeless causes.[38]

Defending pro-Castro Cubans in Miami, in a criminal case utterly suffused with political overtones, with the US government wholly determined to nail a bunch of commies, is a task on a par with conducting a ground war with Russia in the wintertime.

Even in the absence of known anti-Castro Cuban exiles on the jury, the huge influence the exiles have on the rest of the community is an inescapable fact of life in Miami, a place where the sound of the word "pro-Castro" does what the word "bomb" does at an airport.

President Bush has assured the world repeatedly that he will not heed the many calls to lift the Cuban trade embargo unless Fidel Castro releases what Washington calls "political prisoners". Bush tells us this while ten Cubans sit in US prisons, guilty essentially of not being the kind of Cubans George W. loves. If a political prisoner can be defined as one kept in custody who, if not for his or her political beliefs and/or associations would be a free person, then the ten Cubans can be regarded as political prisoners.

It all began in September 1998 when the Justice Department accused 14 Cubans in southern Florida of "conspiracy to gather and deliver defense information to aid a foreign government, that is, the Republic of Cuba" and failing to register as agents of a foreign government.[39] Four of the accused were never apprehended and are believed to be living in Cuba. Five of the 10 arrested, having less than true-believer faith in the American—judicial-system, copped plea bargains to avoid harsher penalties and were sentenced to between three and seven years in prison.

The US Attorney said the actions of the accused—who had been under surveillance since 1995—were an attempt "to strike at the very heart of our national security system and our very democratic process".[40] Their actions, added a judge, "place this nation and its inhabitants in great peril".[41]

Such language would appear more suitable for describing the attacks of September 11, 2001 than the wholly innocuous behavior of the accused. To add further to the level of melodrama: in the Criminal Complaint, in the Indictment, in public statements, and in the courtroom, the federal government continuously squeezed out as much mileage as it could from the fact that the Cubans had gone to meetings and taken part in activities of anti-Castro organizations—"duplicitous participation in and manipulation of" these organizations is how it was put.[42]

But this was all for the benefit of media and jury, for there is obviously no law against taking part in an organization you are unsympathetic with; and in the end, after all the propaganda hoopla, the arrestees were never charged with any such offense.

The Cubans did not deny their activities. Their mission in the United States was to act as an early warning system for their homeland because over the years anti-Castro Cuban exiles in the US have carried out literally hundreds of terrorist actions against the island nation, including as recently as 1997 when they planted bombs in Havana hotels. One of the exile groups, Omega 7, headquartered in Union City, New Jersey, was characterized by the FBI in 1980 as "the most dangerous terrorist organization in the United States".[43]

Some exiles were subpoenaed to testify at the trial, which began in December 2000, and defense attorneys threw questions at them about their activities. One witness told of attempts to assassinate Fidel Castro and of setting Cuban buses and vans on fire. Based on their answers, federal prosecutors threatened to bring organized crime charges against any group whose members gave incriminating testimony and the Assistant US Attorney warned that if additional evidence emerged against members of Alpha 66, considered a paramilitary organization, the group would be prosecuted for a "long-standing pattern of attacks on the Cuban government."[44] Cuba has complained for many years that US authorities ignore information Havana makes available about those in the US it claims are financing and plotting violence.[45] None of the exiles who testified at the trial about terrorist actions or the groups they belonged to were in fact prosecuted.

The arrested Cubans were involved in anti-terrorist activities—so cherished by the government of the United States in word—but were acting against the wrong kind of terrorists. Some of what they uncovered about possible terrorist and drug activities of Cuban exiles—including information concerning the 1997 hotel bombings—they actually passed to the FBI, usually delivered via diplomats in Havana. This presumably is what lay behind the statement in the Criminal Complaint that the defendants "attempted manipulation of United States political institutions and government entities through disinformation and pretended cooperation"[46]—i.e., putting every action of the Cuban defendants in the worst possible light.

One of the Cubans, Antonio Guerrero, was employed as a manual laborer at the US naval base in Boca Chica, Florida, near Key West. The prosecution stated that Guerrero had been ordered by Cuba to track the comings and goings of military aircraft in order to detect "unusual exercises, maneuvers, and other activity related to combat readiness".[47] Guerrero's attorney, to emphasize the non-secret nature of such information, pointed out that anyone sitting in a car on US 1 could easily see planes flying in and out of the base.[48]

This particular operation of the Cuban agents is difficult to comprehend, for it is hard to say which was the more improbable: that the US government would undertake another attack against Cuba, or that these Cubans could get timely wind of it in this manner.

The FBI admitted that the Cubans had not penetrated any military bases and that activities at the bases were "never compromised". "They had no successes," declared an FBI spokesperson. The Pentagon added that "there are no indications that they had access to classified information or access to sensitive areas".[49]

These statements did not of course rise from a desire to aid the Cubans' defense, but rather to assure one and all that the various security systems were impenetrable. But, in short, the government was admitting that nothing that could be termed "espionage" had been committed. Nevertheless, three of the defendants were charged with communicating to Cuba "information relating to the national defense of the United States...intending and having reason to believe that the same would be used to the injury of the United States."[50]

The FBI agents who closely surveilled the Cubans for several years did not seem worried about the reports the "espionage agents" were sending to Havana and made no attempt to thwart their transmission. Indeed, the FBI reportedly arrested the Cubans only because they feared that the group would flee the country following the theft of a computer and disks used by one of them, which contained information about their activities, and that all the FBI surveillance would then have been for nought.[51]

Somewhat more plausibly, those arrested were each charged with "acting as an unregistered agent of a foreign government, Cuba." Yet, in at least the previous five years, no one in the United States had been charged with any such offense, although, given the broad definition in the law of "foreign agent", the Justice Department could have undoubtedly done so with numerous individuals if it had had a political motivation as in this case.[52]

In addition to the unregistered foreign agent charge, which was imposed against all five defendants, there was the ritual laundry list of other charges that is usually facile for a prosecutor to come up with: passport fraud, false passport application, fraudulent identification, conspiracy to defraud the United States, aiding and abetting one or more of the other defendants (sic), conspiracy to commit espionage, and furthermore tacked onto all five—*conspiracy* to act as an unregistered foreign agent.

There was one serious charge, which was levied eight months after the arrests against the alleged leader of the Cuban group, Gerardo Hernández: conspiring to commit murder, a reference to the February 24, 1996 shootdown by a Cuban warplane of two planes (of a total of three), which took the lives of four Miami-based civilian pilots, members of Brothers to the Rescue (BTTR). In actuality, the Cuban government may have done no more than any other government in the world would have done under the same circumstances. The planes were determined to be within Cuban airspace, of serious hostile intent, and Cuban authorities gave the pilots explicit warning: "You are taking a risk." Indeed, both Cuban and US authorities had for some time been giving BTTR—which patrolled the sea between Florida and Cuba looking for refugees—similar warnings about intruding into Cuban airspace.[53]

Jose Basulto, the head of BTTR, and the pilot of the plane that got away, testified at the trial that he had received warnings that Cuba would shoot down planes violating its airspace.[54] In 1995, he had taken an NBC cameraman on a rooftop-level flight over downtown Havana and rained propaganda and religious medals on the streets below, the medals capable of injuring people they struck.[55] Basulto—a long-time CIA collaborator who once fired powerful cannonballs into a Cuban hotel filled with people [56]—described one BTTR flight over Havana as "an act of civil disobedience".[57] His organization's planes had gone into Cuban territory on nine occasions during the previous two years with the pilots being warned repeatedly by Cuba not to return, that they would be shot down if they persisted in carrying out "provocative" flights. A former US federal aviation investigator testified at the trial that in the 1996 incident the planes had ignored warnings and entered an area that was activated as a "danger area".[58]

Also testifying was a retired US Air Force colonel and former regional commander of the North American Air Defense Command (NORAD), George Buchner. Citing National Security Agency transcripts of conversations between a Cuban battle commander on the ground and the Cuban MiG pilots in the air, he stated that the two planes were "well within Cuban airspace" and that a Cuban pilot "showed restraint" by breaking off his pursuit of the third plane as the chase headed toward international airspace.

Buchner's conclusion was at odds with earlier analyses conducted by the United States and the International Civil Aviation Organization (which relied heavily on intelligence data provided by the US). However, he added that the three planes were acting as one and that Cuba was within its sovereign rights to attack them—even in international airspace—because the plane that got away had entered Cuban airspace, a fact not disputed by the prosecution or other investigators.

"The trigger," said Buchner, "was when the first aircraft crossed the 12-mile territorial limit. That allowed the government of Cuba to exercise their sovereign right to protect its airspace." He stated, moreover, that the BTTR planes had given up their civilian status because they still carried the markings of the US Air Force and had been used to drop leaflets condemning the Cuban government.[59]

Two days after the incident, the *New York Times* reported that "United States intelligence officials said that at least one of the American aircraft—the lead plane, which returned safely to Florida—and perhaps all three had violated Cuban airspace." United States officials agreed with the Cuban government that "the pilots had ignored a direct warning from the air traffic control tower in Havana".[60]

Hernández was charged with murder for allegedly giving Cuban authorities the flight plan of the planes flown by Brothers to the Rescue.[61] Even if true, the claim appears to be rather meaningless, for the Federal Aviation Administration (FAA) stated after the incident that after BTTR had filed its flight plan with their agency, it was then transmitted electronically to the air tower in Havana.[62] In any event, on that fateful day in February, when the three planes crossed the 24th parallel—the beginning of the area before entering Cuba's 12-mile territorial limit, which the Cuban government, like other governments, defines as an air-defense identification zone—Basulto radioed his presence to the Havana Air Control Center and his intention to continue further south. Havana, which was already monitoring the planes' flight, replied: "We inform you that the area north of Havana is activated [air defense readied]. You are taking a risk by flying south of twenty-four."[63]

Hernández was also accused of informing Havana, in response to a request, that none of the Cuban agents would be aboard the BTTR planes during the time period in question; one of them had flown with BTTR earlier. This too was equated in the indictment with "knowingly...to perpetrate murder, that is, the unlawful killing of human beings with malice aforethought".[64]

In the final analysis, the planes were shot down for entering Cuban airspace, for purposes hostile, after ignoring many warnings from two governments. After a January 13, 1996 BTTR overflight, Castro had issued orders to his Air Force to shoot down any plane that entered Cuban airspace illegally.[65] And just two weeks prior to the shootdown, a delegation of retired US officials had returned from Havana warning that Cuba seemed prepared to blow the Brothers' Cessnas out of the sky.[66] Gerardo Hernández was not responsible for any of this, and there was, moreover, a long history of planes departing from the United States for Cuba to carry out bombing, strafing, invasion, assassination, subversion, weapon drops, agricultural and industrial sabotage, and other belligerent missions.[67]

According to a former member of BTTR—who redefected to Cuba and may have been a Cuban agent all along—Basulto discussed with him ways to bring explosives into Cuba to blow up high tension wires critical to the country's electrical system and plans to smuggle weapons into Cuba to use in attacks against leaders, including Fidel Castro.[68] At the time of the shootdown, Cuba had been under a 37-year state of siege and could never be sure what such enemy pilots intended to do.

Yet Hernández was sentenced to spend the rest of his life in prison. Ramón Labañino and Antonio Guerrero, the manual worker at the US naval base, were also sentenced to life terms; they and Hernández were all found guilty of conspiracy to commit espionage. Fernando González was put away for 19 1/2 years, and René González received 15 years. All five were convicted of acting as an unregistered agent of a foreign government as well as *conspiracy*—that great redundancy tool that is the lifeblood of American prosecutors—to do the same. All but one had the laundry list of identification frauds thrown at them.

For most of their detention since being arrested, the five men have been kept in solitary confinement. After their convictions, they were placed in five different prisons spread around the country—Pennsylvania, California, Texas, Wisconsin and Colorado—making it difficult for supporters and attorneys to visit more than one. The wife and five-year-old daughter of René González were denied visas to enter the United States from Cuba to visit him. Hernández's wife was already at the Houston airport with all her papers in hand when she was turned back, although not before undergoing several hours of FBI humiliation.

The United States is currently engaged in a worldwide, open-ended, supra-legal campaign to destroy the rights of any individuals who—on the most questionable of evidence or literally none at all—might conceivably represent any kind of terrorist threat.

But if the Cubans—with a much longer history of serious terrorist attacks against them by well known perpetrators—take the most reasonable steps to protect themselves from further attacks, they find that Washington has forbidden them from taking part in the War Against Terrorism. This is particularly ironic given that the same anti-Castro exiles have committed numerous terrorist acts in the United States itself.

CHAPTER FOUR

MICHAEL PARENTI

Michael Parenti is considered one of the U.S. leading progressive thinkers. He received his Ph.D. in political science from Yale University in 1962, and has taught at a number of colleges and universities. His writings have been featured in scholarly journals, popular periodicals, and newspapers, and have been translated into Spanish, Chinese, Japanese, Polish, Portuguese, German, Turkish, and Bangla.

Dr. Parenti lectures around the country on college campuses and before religious, labor, community, peace, and public interest groups. He has appeared on radio and television talk shows to discuss current issues or ideas from his published works.

Michael Parenti is also a historian who has authored 18 books and over 250 articles. His most recent books are *The Assassination of Julius Caesar* (2003) and *Superpatriotism* (2004).

Aggression and Propaganda Against Cuba

The grave injustices perpetrated by the US government against the Cuban Five can best be understood if framed in the historical context of US-Cuban relations. For the better part of four decades Washington policymakers have treated Cuba with unrelieved antagonism. Why so? During that time, U.S. rulers and their faithful acolytes in the major media have propagated every sort of misrepresentation to mislead the world as regards their policy of aggression toward Cuba. Why?

Defending Global Capitalism

In June 1959, some five months after the triumph of the Cuban Revolution, the Havana government promulgated an agrarian reform law that provided for state appropriation of large private landholdings. Under this law, US sugar corporations eventually lost about 1,666,000 acres of choice land and many millions of dollars in future cash-crop exports. The following year, President Dwight Eisenhower, citing Havana's "hostility" toward the United States, cut Cuba's sugar quota by about 95 percent, in effect imposing a total boycott on publicly produced Cuban sugar. Three months later, in October 1959, the Cuban government nationalized all banks and large commercial and industrial enterprises, including the many that belonged to US firms.

Cuba's move away from a free-market system dominated by US firms and toward a not-for-profit socialist economy caused it to become the target of an unremitting series of attacks perpetrated by the US national security state. These attacks included U.S.-sponsored sabotage, espionage, terrorism, trade sanctions, embargo, and outright invasion. The purpose behind this aggression was to undermine the Revolution and deliver Cuba safely back to the tender mercies of global capitalism.

The U.S. policy toward Cuba has been consistent with its longstanding policy of trying to subvert any country that pursues an alternative path in the use of its land, labor, capital, markets, and natural resources. Any country or political movement that emphasizes self-development, egalitarian human services, and public ownership is condemned as an enemy of the USA and targeted for sanctions or other forms of attack. In contrast, the countries deemed "friendly toward America" and "pro-West" are those that leave themselves at the disposal of large U.S. investors on terms that are totally favorable to the moneyed corporate interests.

Of course, this is not what U.S. rulers tell the people of North America. As early as July 1960, the White House charged that Cuba was "hostile" to the United States (despite the Cuban government's repeated overtures for normal friendly relations). The Castro government, in Eisenhower's words, was "dominated by international communism."[1] Cuba was a threat to the "stability" of the hemisphere and to the survival of American democracy, we heard. U.S. officials repeatedly charged that the island government was a cruel dictatorship and that the United States had no choice but to try "restoring" Cuban liberty.

U.S. rulers never explained why they were so suddenly concerned about the freedoms of the Cuban people. In the two decades before the Revolution, successive administrations in Washington manifested no opposition to the brutally repressive autocracy headed by General Fulgencio Batista. Quite the contrary, they sent him military aid, did a vigorous business with him, and treated him well in every other way. The significant but unspoken difference between Castro and Batista was that Batista, a comprador ruler, left Cuba wide open to U.S. capital penetration. In contrast, Castro and his revolutionary movement did away with private corporate control of the economy, nationalized U.S. holdings, and renovated the class structure toward a more collectivized and egalitarian mode. That is what made Fidel Castro so insufferable in Washington—and still does.

Needless to say, the U.S. method of mistreatment has been applied to other countries besides Cuba. Numerous potentially dissident regimes that have asked for friendly relations have been met with abuse and aggression from Washington: Vietnam, Chile (under Allende), Mozambique, Angola, Cambodia, Nicaragua (under the Sandinistas), Panama (under Torrijo), Grenada (under the New Jewel Movement), Yugoslavia (under Milosevic), Haiti (under Aristide) Venezuela (under Chavez), and numerous others.[2] The U.S. modus operandi is:

- to heap criticism on the targeted government for imprisoning the butchers, assassins, terrorists, and torturers of the previous U.S.-backed reactionary regime;
- denounce the revolutionary or reformist government as "totalitarian" for failing to immediately institute Western-style, electoral politics;
- launch *ad hominem* attacks upon the leader, labeling him as fanatical, brutal, repressive, genocidal, power hungry, or even mentally imbalanced;
- denounce the country as a threat to regional peace and stability;
- harass, destabilize, and impose economic sanctions to cripple its economy;
- attack it with surrogate forces, trained, equipped and financed by the CIA and led by members of the former regime, or even with regular U.S. armed forces.

Manipulating Public Opinion

How the corporate-owned capitalist press has served in the crusade against Cuba tells us a lot about why the U.S. public is so misinformed about issues relating to that country. Following the official White House line, the corporate news media regularly denied that the United States harbored aggressive designs against Cuba or any other government. The stance taken against Cuba, it was said, was simply a defense against Communist aggrandizement. Cuba was repeatedly condemned as a tool of Soviet aggression and expansionism. But now that the Soviet Union no longer exists, Cuba is still treated as a mortal enemy. U.S. acts of aggression—including armed invasion itself—continue to be magically transformed into acts of defense. We have seen this legerdemain time and again, most recently in the aggression against Iraq.

Consider the Bay of Pigs. In April 1961, about 1,600 right-wing Cuban émigrés, trained and financed by the CIA, and assisted by hundreds of U.S. "advisors," invaded Cuba. In the words of one of their leaders, their intent was to overthrow Castro and set up "a provisional government" that "will restore all properties to the rightful owners."[3] Reports of the impending invasion circulated widely throughout Central America. In the United States, however, where there reputedly exists the freest press in the world, few people were informed. The mounting evidence of an impending invasion was suppressed by the Associated Press and United Press International and by all the major newspapers and newsweeklies, seventy-five of whom—in an impressively unanimous act of self-censorship—rejected a story offered by the editors of the Nation (a small circulation liberal weekly) detailing U.S. preparations for the invasion.[4]

Fidel Castro's accusation that U.S. rulers were planning to invade Cuba was dismissed by the New York Times as "shrill...anti-American propaganda," and by Time magazine as Castro's "continued tawdry little melodrama of invasion."[5] When Washington broke diplomatic relations with Cuba in January 1961, the New York Times explained, "What snapped U.S. patience was a new propaganda offense from Havana charging that the U.S. was plotting an 'imminent invasion' of Cuba."[6] How ridiculous of Havana to entertain such suspicions. Yet in fact, the Bay of Pigs invasion proved to be something more than a figment of Fidel Castro's imagination.

Such is the predominance of the anti-Communist orthodoxy in U.S. public life that, after the Bay of Pigs, there was a total lack of critical discussion among U.S. political figures and media commentators regarding the moral and legal impropriety of the invasion. Instead commentary focused exclusively on tactical questions. There were repeated references to the disappointing "fiasco" and "disastrous attempt" and the need to free Cuba from the "Communist yoke." It was never acknowledged that the invasion failed not because of "insufficient air coverage," as some of the invaders claimed, but because the Cuban people, instead of rising to join the counterrevolutionary expeditionary force as anticipated by U.S. leaders, closed ranks behind their Revolution.

Among the Cuban-exile invaders taken prisoner near *Bahia de los Cochinos* were men who between them had previously owned in Cuba 914,859 acres of land, 9666 houses, 70 factories, 5 mines, 2 banks, and 10 sugar mills.[7] They were the scions of the privileged propertied class of pre-revolutionary Cuba, coming back to reclaim their substantial holdings. But in the U.S. media they were represented as nothing other than "freedom fighters," dedicated champions of liberty—who had lived so comfortably and uncomplainingly under the Batista dictatorship.

Why would the Cuban people stand by the "Castro dictatorship"? That was never explained in the United States. Not a word appeared in the U.S. press about the advances made by ordinary Cubans under the Revolution, the millions who for the first time had access to education, literacy, medical care, decent housing, jobs with adequate pay and good work conditions, and a host of other public services—all of which are far from perfect but still offering a better life than the free-market misery endured under the U.S.-Batista ancient régime.

Avoiding Better Relations

Because of the U.S. embargo, Cuba has the highest import-export tonnage costs of any country in the world, having to buy its school buses and medical supplies all the way from Japan and other far-off places rather than from the nearby United States.

Better relations with the USA would bring the Cubans more trade, technology, and tourism, and the chance to cut their defense expenditures. Yet Havana's overtures for friendlier relations have been repeatedly rebuffed by successive administrations in Washington.

Not too long ago, when Havana announced plans to construct a nonmilitary nuclear plant, U.S. rulers muttered ominously about Cuba's "potential nuclear threat." During the 2001-2004 period, under the administration of George W. Bush, relations went from bad to worse. The U.S. interest section in Havana was caught engaging in organizing counterrevolutionary activity. As part of Washington's attempt to reduce hard currency in Cuba, Cuban-Americans who visited the island were obliged to take fewer U.S. dollars than before.[8] Overall restrictions on travel to Cuba became more stringent. And in early 2003 U.S. pundits were openly talking about invading Cuba—a discussion that was put on hold only after the invasion of Iraq proved so difficult and costly.

If the U.S. government justifies its own hostility on the grounds that Cuba is hostile toward the United States, what becomes the justification when the Cuban government tries to be friendly? The response is to emphasize the negative. Even when reporting the cordial overtures made by Cuba, U.S. media pundits and Washington policymakers perpetuate the stereotype of a sinister "Marxist regime" as the manipulative aggressor. In 1984 the New York Times ran a "news analysis" headlined "WHAT'S BEHIND CASTRO'S SOFTER TONE." The headline itself suggested that Castro was up to something. The opening sentence read, "Once again Fidel Castro is talking as if he wants to improve relations with the United States" ("as if" not actually). According to the Times, Castro was interested in "taking advantage" of U.S. trade, technology, and tourism and would "prefer not to be spending so much time and energy on national defense." Here seemed to be a promising basis for improved relations.

Fidel Castro was saying that Cuba's own self-interest rested on friendlier diplomatic and economic ties with Washington and not, as the United States claimed, on military buildups and aggressive confrontations. Nevertheless, the Times analysis made nothing of Castro's stated desire to ease tensions and instead presented the rest of the story from the U.S. government's perspective. It noted that most Washington officials "seem skeptical.... The Administration continues to believe that the best way to deal with the Cuban leader is with unyielding firmness.... Administration officials see little advantage in wavering."[9]

The article did not explain what justified this "skeptical" stance, nor why a blanket negative response to Castro should be described as "unyielding firmness" rather than, say, "unyielding rigidity." Nor did it say why a willingness to respond seriously to his overture must be labeled "wavering." The impressions left is that the power-hungry Castro was out to get something from us but our leaders weren't about to be taken in. There was no mention of what the United States had to lose if it entered friendlier relations with Cuba.

In short, the U.S. stance was immune to evidence. If the Cubans condemn U.S. aggressions, this is proof of their hostility and diabolic design. If they act in a friendly manner and ask for negotiated settlements, showing a willingness to make concessions, then it is assumed they are up to something and are resorting to deceptively manipulative ploys. The U.S. position is nonfalsifiable: both A and not-A become proof of the same thing.

"Democracy" and Its Double Standards

U.S. policymakers have long condemned Cuba for its controlled press. The Cubans, we are told, are subjected to a totalitarian indoctrination and do not enjoy the diverse and open discourse that is said to be found in the "free and independent"

U.S. media. In fact, the average Cuban has more access to Western news sources than the average American has to Cuban sources. (The same was true of the former Soviet Union. In 1985 Soviet leader Mikhail Gorbachev pointed out that U.S. television programs, movies, books, music, and magazines were in relative abundance in the USSR compared to the almost nonexistent supply of Soviet films and publications in the United States. He offered to stop jamming Voice of America broadcasts to his country if Washington would allow normal frequency transmission of Radio Moscow to the USA, an offer the U.S. government declined.)

Likewise, Cuba is bombarded with U.S. broadcasting, including Voice of America, regular Spanish-language stations from Miami, and a U.S.-sponsored propaganda station called "Radio Marti." Havana has asked that Cuba be allowed a frequency for Cuban use in the United States, something Washington has refused to do. In response to those who attack the lack of dissent in the Cuban media, Fidel Castro has promised to open up the Cuban press to all opponents of the Revolution on the day he saw U.S. Communists enjoying regular access to the U.S. major media.[10] Needless to say, U.S. rulers have never taken up the offer.

Cuba has also been condemned for not allowing its people to flee the island. That so many want to leave Cuba is treated as proof that Cuban socialism is a harshly repressive system, rather than that the U.S. embargo has made life difficult in Cuba. That so many millions more want to leave capitalist countries like Mexico, Nigeria, Poland, El Salvador, Philippines, South Korea, Macedonia, and too many others to list is never treated as grounds for questioning the capitalist free-market system that inflicts such misery upon the Third World.

In accordance with an agreement between Havana and Washington, the Cuban government allowed people to leave for the United States if they had a U.S. visa. Washington had agreed to issue 20,000 visas a year but in fact granted few, preferring to incite illegal departures and reap the propaganda value. Cubans who fled illegally on skimpy crafts or hijacked vessels and planes were hailed as heroes who had risked their lives to flee Castro's tyranny, and were granted asylum in the USA. When Havana announced it would let anyone leave who wanted to, the Clinton administration reverted to a closed-door policy, fearing an immigration tide. Now policymakers voiced concern that the escape of too many disgruntled refugees would help Castro stay in power by easing tensions within Cuban society. In brief, Cuba was condemned for not allowing its citizens to leave and then for allowing them to leave.

No Full Circle

Lacking a class perspective, all sorts of experts come to conclusions about Cuba based on surface appearances. While attending a World Affairs Council meeting in San Francisco, I heard some participants refer to the irony of Cuba's having come "full circle" since the days before the Revolution. In pre-revolutionary Cuba, the best hotels and shops were reserved for the foreigners and the relatively few Cubans who had Yankee dollars. Today, it is the same, these experts gleefully observed.

This judgment overlooks some important differences. Strapped for hard currency, the revolutionary government decided to take advantage of its beautiful beaches and sunny climate to develop a tourist industry. Today, tourism is one of Cuba's most important sources of hard currency income, if not the most important. True, tourists are given accommodations that most Cubans cannot afford. But in pre-revolutionary Cuba, the profits from tourism were pocketed by big corporations, generals, gamblers, and mobsters. Today the profits are split between the foreign investors who build and manage the hotels and the Cuban government. The portion going to the government helps to pay for health clinics, education, machinery, powdered milk, the importation of fuel, and the like. In other words, the people reap much of the benefits of the tourist trade—as is true of the export earnings from Cuban sugar, coffee, tobacco, rum, seafood, honey, nickel, and marble.

If Cuba were in exactly the same place as before the Revolution, completely under client-state servitude, Washington would have lifted the embargo and embraced Havana, as it has done to some degree with China and Vietnam—both of whom are energetically encouraging the growth of a low-wage, private investment sector. When the Cuban government no longer utilizes the public sector to redistribute a major portion of the surplus value to the common populace, when it allows the surplus wealth to be pocketed by a few rich corporate owners, and when it returns the factories and lands to an opulent owning class—as the former Communist governments of Eastern Europe have done—then will it have come full circle, returning to a privatized, free-market, client-state servitude. And only then will it be warmly embraced by Washington—as have the ex-Communist Eastern European nations.

In 1994 I wrote a letter to Representative Lee Hamilton, Chair of the House Foreign Affairs Committee, urging a normalization of relations with Cuba. He wrote back that U.S. policy toward Cuba should be "updated" in order to be more effective, and that "we must put Cuba in contact with the ideas and practice of democracy…and the economic benefits of a free market system." The embargo, Hamilton went on, was put in place to "promote democratic change in Cuba and retaliate for the large-scale seizure of American assets by the Castro regime."

Needless to say, Hamilton did not explain why his own government—which had supported a pre-revolutionary dictatorship in Cuba for generations—was now so insistent on installing U.S.-style democracy on the island. The revealing thing in his letter was his acknowledgment that Washington's policy was dedicated to advancing the cause of the "free market system" and retaliating for the "large-scale seizure of American assets." In so many words, he was letting us know that a fundamental commitment of U.S. policy was to make the world safe for corporate investments and profits.

Those who do not believe that U.S. rulers are consciously dedicated to the propagation of capitalism should note how policymakers now explicitly demand "free-market reforms" in one country after another. We no longer have to impute such intentions to them. Almost all their actions and—with increasing frequency—their own words testify to what they have been doing. When forced to choose between democracy without capitalism or capitalism without democracy, U.S. rulers unhesitatingly embrace the latter—although they also prefer the legitimating cloak of a limited and well-controlled "democracy" when possible.

Likewise in the case of the Cuban Five, when obliged to choose between fair play for the accused or repression in defense of U.S. corporate rule, they go for repression. The enemies of peace and justice are not in Havana; they are in Washington.

CHAPTER FIVE

PIERO GLEIJESES

Piero Gleijeses is Professor of American Foreign Policy at Johns Hopkins University. He has published *Conflicting Missions: Havana, Washington and Africa, 1959–1976* (2002), which won the 2002 Robert Ferrell Prize from the Society for Historians of American Foreign Relations; Shattered Hope: The Guatemalan Revolution and the United States (1991); Politics and Culture in Guatemala (1988); Tilting at Windmills: Reagan in Central America (1982); The Dominican Crisis: The 1965 Constitutionalist Revolt and American Intervention (1978).

Cuba, Africa and the Cuban Five

At a round table in Havana in January 2004 the South African ambassador to Cuba reflected on the events that led to the independence of Namibia and the gradual withdrawal of the Cuban troops from Angola in the late 1980s. "In a small village called Cuito Cuanavale [in southeastern Angola]," she said, "Cuban, Angolan and Namibian troops defeated the South African army. The story of southern Africa...changed dramatically from that moment on. A paralyzing blow—from which they were never to recover—was struck to the last bastion of colonialism in Africa...The gates of freedom were opened, starting with Namibia and followed by South Africa years later. The key component to this defeat was the internationalism of Cuba and its people."[1]

Cuba's contribution to the struggle against apartheid, which Castro has called "the most beautiful cause,"[2] had begun well before the battle of Cuito Cuanavale. "I was in prison when I first heard [in 1975] of the massive aid that the internationalist

Cuban troops were giving to the people of Angola," Nelson Mandela recalled in 1991. "We in Africa are accustomed to being the victims of countries that want to grab our territory or subvert our sovereignty. In all the history of Africa this is the only time a foreign people has risen up to defend one of our countries."[3]

I want to revisit these momentous events—when Cuba's troops first arrived in Angola in the mid-1970s, and when Cuba's troops defeated the South Africans at Cuito Cuanavale in the late 1980s. Even though these actions were not, formally, part of the indictment against Gerardo Hernández and his friends, they are among the sins for which these five heroes have to pay.

The basic outline of what happened in 1975-76 is well known and requires little elaboration here; I will examine instead the impact. The events of 1987-88 are far less well known, and it will be necessary first to establish what happened before analyzing the repercussions.[4]

Upon the collapse of the Portuguese dictatorship on April 25, 1974, there were three rival independence movements in Angola: Agostinho Neto's Popular Movement for the Liberation of Angola (MPLA), Holden Roberto's National Front for the Liberation of Angola (FNLA), and Jonas Savimbi's National Union for the Total Independence of Angola (UNITA). On January 15, 1975, Portugal and these three movements agreed that a transitional government, under a Portuguese High Commissioner, would rule the country until independence on November 11, 1975. In the meantime, there would be elections for a Constituent Assembly which would elect Angola's first president.

But civil war erupted in the spring of 1975. As independence day approached, the MPLA was winning, defeating the FNLA-UNITA coalition. Not because of Cuban aid—no Cubans were fighting yet in Angola. Not because of superiority in weapons—the rival coalition had a slight edge, thanks to US and South African largesse. It was winning because, as the CIA station chief in Luanda noted, it was by far the most disciplined and committed of the three movements. The MPLA leaders "were more effective, better educated, better trained and better motivated" than those of the FNLA and UNITA. "The rank and file also were better motivated."[5] It was to prevent this MPLA victory that South African troops—a column named Zulu—invaded Angola on October 14, transforming the civil war into an international conflict. South Africa was well aware of Neto's implacable hostility to apartheid and of his commitment to assist the liberation movements of southern Africa. Still, Pretoria might have hesitated had Washington not egged it on. Secretary of State Henry Kissinger had decided that Angola could provide a cheap boost to the prestige of the United States, and to his own prestige, pummeled by the fall of South Vietnam the previous April. He cast the struggle in bold Cold War terms: the FNLA and UNITA would crush the Soviet-backed MPLA. (In fact Soviet aid to the MPLA was very limited because Moscow distrusted Neto and did not want to jeopardize the SALT II treaty negotiations.)

As the South Africans raced toward Luanda, MPLA resistance crumbled. Zulu would have seized the city had Castro not decided, on November 4, to send troops in response to the MPLA's desperate appeals. The Cubans halted the South African advance, and then pushed Zulu back until, on March 27, 1976, the last South African troops withdrew.

It is now beyond question that, as a Soviet official states in his memoirs, the Cubans sent their troops "on their own initiative and without consulting us."[6] Indeed the evidence is so compelling that even Kissinger, who habitually dismissed the Cubans as Soviet proxies, has reconsidered. "At the time we thought he [Castro] was operating as a Soviet surrogate," he writes in the final volume of his memoirs. "We could not imagine that he would act so provocatively so far from home unless he was pressured by Moscow to repay the Soviet Union for its military and economic support. Evidence now available suggests that the opposite was the case."[7]

What, then, motivated Castro's bold move in Angola? Not Cuba's narrow interests; not realpolitik. By deciding to send troops Castro challenged Moscow, for he knew that Brezhnev opposed the move. He faced a serious military risk: Pretoria, urged on by Washington and possibly Paris, might have escalated its involvement, and Castro's soldiers might have faced the full fury of the South African army without any guarantee of Soviet assistance. (Indeed, it took two months for Moscow to begin to provide much needed logistical support to the airlift of Cuban troops to Angola.) Furthermore, the dispatch of Cuban troops jeopardized relations with the West at a moment when they were improving markedly: the United States was probing a modus vivendi; the Organization of American States had just lifted its sanctions; and the West European governments were offering Havana low-interest loans and development aid.

Realpolitik would have demanded that Cuba refuse Luanda's appeals. Had he been a client of the Soviet Union, Castro would have held back.

What motivated the decision to send troops was idealism. The victory of the Pretoria-Washington axis would have meant the victory of apartheid, the tightening of the grip of white domination over the people of southern Africa. It was a defining moment. Castro sent his soldiers. As Kissinger himself now says: Castro "was probably the most genuine revolutionary leader then in power."[8]

Cuba's victory prevented the establishment of a government in Luanda beholden to the apartheid regime. The tidal wave unleashed by the Cuban victory washed over southern Africa. Its psychological impact, the hope it aroused, is aptly illustrated by two statements from across the political divide in South Africa. In February 1976, as the Cuban troops were pushing the South

African army toward the Namibian border, a South African military analyst wrote: "In Angola Black troops—Cubans and Angolans—have defeated White troops in military exchanges. Whether the bulk of the offensive was by Cubans or Angolans is immaterial in the color-conscious context of this war's battlefield, for the reality is that they won, are winning, and are not White; and that psychological edge, that advantage the White man has enjoyed and exploited over 300 years of colonialism and empire, is slipping away. White elitism has suffered an irreversible blow in Angola, and Whites who have been there know it."[9] The "White Giants" had retreated for the first time in recent history—and black Africans celebrated. "Black Africa is riding the crest of a wave generated by the Cuban success in Angola," noted the *World*, South Africa's major black newspaper. "Black Africa is tasting the heady wine of the possibility of realizing the dream of total liberation."[10] There would have been no heady dream, but rather the pain of crushing defeat, had the Cubans not intervened.

The impact was more than moral. It had clear, tangible consequences throughout southern Africa. It forced Kissinger to turn against the racist white regime in Rhodesia and kept Carter on the narrow good path until Zimbabwe was finally born in 1980.[11] And it marked the real beginning of Namibia's war of independence. As a South African general writes, "For the first time they [the Namibian rebels] obtained what is more or less a prerequisite for successful insurgent campaigning, namely a border that provided safe refuge."[12] For twelve years—until the New York agreements of December 1988—Pretoria refused to leave Namibia, and Cuban troops helped the Angolan army hold the line against bruising South African incursions into Angola.

Very little has been written about those years. The major published source is the memoirs of Reagan's assistant secretary for African affairs, Chester Crocker, who explains the outcome—the independence of Namibia—largely in terms of US patience, skill and wisdom.[13] A different explanation emerges from an analysis of newly declassified Cuban and US documents. In April 1987, the US ambassador reported from Pretoria that the South African government was "implacably negative" toward Namibian independence.[14] The following September the South African Defense Force (SADF) unleashed a major attack against the Angolan army in southeastern Angola. By early November it had cornered the best Angolan units in the small town of Cuito Cuanavale and was poised to destroy them. Pretoria's aggression was so brazen that on November 25, in a unanimous vote, the UN Security Council demanded that South Africa "unconditionally withdraw all its forces occupying Angolan territory."[15] Crocker reassured the South African ambassador to the United States, "The SAG [South African Government] should take note that the resolution did not contain a call for comprehensive sanctions, and did not provide for any assistance to Angola. That was no accident, but a consequence of our own efforts to keep the resolution within bounds."[16] In the meantime, Pretoria was annihilating the elite units of the Angolan army. By mid-January 1988 South African military sources and western diplomats were announcing that the fall of Cuito was "imminent."[17]

But Cuito did not fall. On November 15, 1987, Castro had ordered the best units of his army and its most sophisticated hardware to Angola. Castro intended to do much more than save Cuito Cuanavale: he wanted to force the SADF out of Angola. "By going there [to Cuito Cuanavale] we placed ourselves in the lion's jaws," Castro explained. "We accepted the challenge. And from the first moment we planned to gather our forces to attack in another direction, like a boxer who with his left hand blocks the blow and with his right—strikes."[18] As in 1975, Castro had not consulted Moscow. As he well understood, the Soviets, who were focused on the detente with the United States, were wary of any action that might lead to a military escalation in southern

Africa.[19]

On March 23, 1988, the South African army launched its last major attack against Cuito. It was "brought to a grinding and definite halt" by the defenders, an SADF officer writes.[20] Three days later, Soviet Deputy Foreign Minister Anatoly Adamishin arrived in Havana to brief the Cubans on recent Soviet conversations in Washington with President Ronald Reagan, Secretary of State George Shultz, and Chester Crocker. Based on his talks with the South African foreign minister, Crocker had warned Adamishin that "South Africa will not withdraw from Angola until the Cuban troops have left the country." Crocker had also said that the South African military, which was increasingly influential in policy-making, "feel every day more comfortable in Angola, where they are able to try out new weapons and inflict severe blows on the Angolan army." The message was clear: if Havana and Luanda wanted Pretoria to withdraw from Angola they would have to agree to significant concessions.[21]

Castro was not impressed: "One should ask [the Americans]," he told Adamishin, "If the South Africans are so powerful...why haven't they been able to take Cuito? It has been four months since they have arrived at the doors of Cuito Cuanavale. Why has the army of the superior race been unable to take Cuito, which is defended by black and mulattoes from Angola and the Caribbean?"[22]

As he spoke, hundreds of miles southwest of Cuito a Cuban army had begun to advance toward the Namibian border. "At any other time," US intelligence reported, "Pretoria would have regarded the Cuban move as a provocation, requiring a swift and strong response. But the Cubans moved with such dispatch and on such a scale that an immediate South African military response would have involved serious risks."[23] The South Africans fulminated, warning that the Cuban advance posed a "serious" military threat to Namibia and that it could precipitate "a terrible battle."[24] But they gave ground.

Among the Cuban soldiers advancing toward the Namibian border were two young men whose names are now well known: Fernando González Llort y Gerardo Hernández Nordelo. Ten years earlier, René González Sehweren had also fought in Angola. These three men, together with Ramón Labañino Salazar y Antonio Guerrero Rodríguez, are the five Cubans honored in this book.

While Castro's troops advanced toward the Namibian border, Cubans, Angolans, South Africans and Americans were sparring at the negotiating table.

Throughout, the Soviets remained on the sidelines. US intelligence observed, "The Soviets seem to want an early resolution, but have so far only offered vague and tentative ideas regarding the forms it might take. They are still unprepared to press their allies." The South African president, P.W. Botha, who for years had delighted in depicting the Cubans as Soviet proxies, told his parliament that Mikhail Gorbachev wanted peace, but "it is not clear to what extent the Russians can influence President Castro." The truth was: not much. The Soviet Union was not ready to apply pressure on its proud ally. Anatoly Dobrynin, the long-time Soviet ambassador to the United States, deferred to Jorge Risquet, Castro's point man for Africa: "You have the leading role in these negotiations," he told him.[25]

For South Africans and Americans the big questions was: What will the Cubans do? Would they stop at the Namibian border? It was to answer this question that Crocker sought out Risquet. "My question is the following," he said: "Does Cuba intend to halt the advance of its troops at the border between Namibia and Angola?' Risquet replied, "I have no answer for you. I cannot give a Meprobamato [a well-known Cuban tranquillizer]—not to you and not to the South Africans.... I have not said whether or not our troops will stop. .... Listen to me, I am not threatening. If I told you that they will not stop, it would be a threat. If I told you that they will stop, I would be giving you a Meprobamato, a Tylenol, and I want neither to threaten you nor to give you a tranquillizer... What I have said is that the only guarantee [that our troops will stop at the border] would be an agreement [on the independence of Namibia]."[26]

The next day, Cuban planes attacked a SADF position at Calueque, seven miles north of the border. "It was a very deliberate, well-planned attack," a South African colonel recalled. The CIA reported: "Cuba's successful use of air power and the apparent weakness of Pretoria's air defenses...illustrate the dilemma Pretoria faces in confronting the Cuban challenge. South African forces can inflict serious damage on selected Cuban-Angolan units, but Cuba retains advantages, particularly in air defenses and the number of aircraft and troops."[27] Until that moment, US intelligence had said that Pretoria retained air superiority. This precious weapon, Pretoria's edge through all the years of the conflict, was now gone. Havana had achieved air superiority over southern Angola and northern Namibia. A few hours after the Cubans' successful strike against Calueque, the SADF destroyed a nearby bridge over the Cunene River. They did so, the CIA surmised, "to deny Cuban and Angolan ground forces easy passage to the Namibia border and to reduce the number of positions they must defend."[28] Never had the danger of a Cuban advance into Namibia seemed more real.

A few days later the South African government received another, painful blow: an editorial in *Die Kerkbode*, the official organ of the biggest of South Africa's Dutch Reformed Churches, expressed disquiet "on Christian-ethical grounds" about the "more or less permanent" presence of the SADF in Angola. "Doubts about the wisdom of the Government's military strategy are not new," the Johannesburg *Star* noted in an editorial. "But what is especially significant about *Die Kerkbode's* querying the ethics of the Angola operations is that the doubts are now being expressed from within the National Party's own constituency. Hardly a revolt, but this subterranean questioning from the guardians of the Afrikaner conscience cannot be easily ignored by government."[29] *Die Kerkbode* argued the case on moral grounds, but the timing—after the South African failure at Cuito, the Cubans' advance toward the Namibian border and their successful strike against Calueque—suggests that more than moral qualms had triggered the editorial.

On July 22, senior Cuban and Angolan military officers met with their South African counterparts and US officials in Cape Verde to discuss a possible cease-fire. After a few hours, the South Africans bowed to the Cubans' demands: they would withdraw all their troops from Angola by September 1 in exchange for an immediate cease-fire.[30] On August 25, while the last SADF troops were preparing to leave Angola, Crocker cabled Shultz after another negotiating round, "Reading the Cubans is yet another art form. They are prepared for both war and peace...We witness considerable tactical finesse and genuinely creative moves at the table. This occurs against the backdrop of Castro's grandiose bluster and his army's unprecedented projection of power on the ground."[31]

The negotiations continued through the fall, while thousands of Cuban soldiers waited within striking distance of Namibia and Cuban planes patrolled the skies. Finally on December 22, in New York, came the dramatic reversal: South Africa accepted the independence of Namibia. Many factors influenced Pretoria, but there would have been no New York agreements without the Cubans' military prowess on the battlefield and their skill at the negotiating table.

This prowess and this skill reverberated beyond Namibia. As Mandela declared when he visited Havana in 1991, the Cuban victory "destroyed the myth of the invincibility of the white oppressor...[and] inspired the fighting masses of South Africa... Cuito Cuanavale was the turning point for the liberation of our continent—and of my people—from the scourge of apartheid.... We come here," he said, "with a sense of the great debt that is owed the people of Cuba.... What other country can point to a record of greater selflessness than Cuba had displayed in its relations to Africa?"[32]

Any fair assessment of Cuba's foreign policy must recognize its impressive successes, and particularly its role in changing the course of southern African history in defiance of Washington's best efforts to stop it. These foreign policy successes explain why, as a former British ambassador in Havana writes, Castro is "still a bone which stuck in American throats. He had defied and mocked the world's only superpower, and would not be forgiven."[33] The desire for revenge, and not just for the Miami vote, explains why the deeply immoral embargo continues. And it explains why five brave Cubans were tried in a kangaroo court and are suffering now in the prisons of the United States.

CHAPTER SIX

IGNACIO RAMONET

Ignacio Ramonet is Professor of Communication Theory at Denis-Diderot University of Paris. He is also the Director of the Paris-based newspaper *Le Monde Diplomatique*. He has published, among other books, *Propagandes silencieuses*, *Géopolitique du chaos* and *La Tyrannie de la communication*.

Miami, a Nest of Terrorists

In July 1981, almost 25 years ago, I was sent on a mission to Florida by *Le Monde Diplomatique* to write an extensive inquiry into the Hispanic community that had become the main *non-wasp* community in the Unites States of America. I had already toured around New York and its environs to meet the Puerto Ricans. Then I went to California and stayed in the Chicano quarter in Los Angeles and San Francisco. Finally, to get to know the Cubans in Florida, I went to Miami, a city suffocating in seasonal heat and humidity.

I relaxed there for a few weeks in a modest air-conditioned bungalow surrounded by a small tropical garden. I had to rent a car because public transport in that city was non-existent. That was the first time I visited Florida. Like all journalists, I had a list of contacts representing the different media. I was advised to be on the alert because there were hard-line factions in the Cuban community, particularly among the anti-Castro groups, that detested journalists, especially French journalists, and, particularly those from *Le Monde Diplomatique*.

At this stage, the hope of returning to live on the island after the collapse of the revolutionary regime had seriously diminished among the Cubans. In Florida, they were adopting US nationality more and more (43. 3% in 1981). In 1965, many Cuban exiles firmly believed that Fidel Castro's regime would be short-lived and would fall quickly because of the US blockade. Later, many resigned themselves to the situation and the majority decided to have not only formal, but also friendly bonds with the country. So from then on, there was an enthusiastic acceptance of the 1977 proposal to visit their relatives in Cuba. Hundreds of thousands of them had already made that journey.

But I could sense that the project to destroy Castro's regime still persisted. For instance, in the Omega 7 secret terrorist organization, even today followers oppose any reconciliation with the Cuban government and promote the necessity of assassination. That group sows terror among those exiles who are in favor of better understanding with Havana. In April 1979, they were responsible for the assassination of Carlos Muñíz Varela, leader of the Antonio Maceo Brigade (Cuban American youngsters who go to Cuba every year to cut sugar cane) and in November of the same year, they assassinated José Eulalio Negrín, another leader of the Cuban community in Miami.

There are other non-secret organizations based in Florida that openly recruited combatants to train in their camps and be sent in regiments to fight in Cuba or assassinate Fidel Castro. The oldest and most significant of those organizations is Alpha 66, founded in 1962 and led by Andrés Nazario Sargén, a former peasant leader that fought against Batista's regime in the Sierra Maestra beside Fidel Castro and later rejected the "road of communism".

I arranged a meeting with Andrés Nazario Sargén. He received me in the late afternoon at the headquarters of Alpha 66, a luxurious house in the South East of Miami, 66, (La Sahuesera), not far form Calle 8 (8th Street) the epicenter of Little Havana. Mr. Nazario was then a man in his fifties, small, a bit over-weight and full of energy, who still had the rustic manners of his peasant origin. He introduced me to his staff, four or five anti-Castro veterans. In my opinion, he behaved in a very friendly way, as hospitable as any other Cuban. He told he could not ignore the fact that in France the majority of newspapers and intellectuals sympathized with the Cuban Revolution, but that he had to tell me how he felt; his version of things.

We passed into a small room where we were served very strong coffee. Nazario recalled his own experiences with Batista as a member of the revolutionary forces. He showed me a photograph with himself and his wife beside the revolutionary commander Camilo Cienfuegos and explained why he had broken with the Cuban Revolution: "I did not fight against one dictatorship to install another" he said, "a Communist lackey under the orders of Moscow. He recalled how it was for him and how he continued as "a fighter all my life". In 1961 he went to Puerto Rico with his friends Diego Medina (who died in 1999), Colonel Vicente Mendez and the Alpha 66 organization, considered one of the most dangerous of all anti-Castro terrorist organizations based in Florida.

He recounted the armed attacks on the Cuban authorities, the assaults on the coast guards and fishing boats ("spies"), the landing in Cuba, the attacks on the hotels in Cayo Coco, on the Youth Hostels in Tarará, etc. He recalled how Alpha 66 had trained the commando group led by Eloy Gutierrez Menoyo in the Dominican Republic, which landed in the Eastern province of Cuba to commit terrorist actions before being arrested.

Nazario Sargén boastfully described the deadly actions, which were completely illegal according to international law. *"Where did you train?"* I asked him. He described a series of grand maneuvers in Florida where his commandos used to meet regularly to learn how to use the surplus US armed forces weapons readily available on the market. He showed me huge color photographs representing the training scenes where you can see some potbellied, retired Cuban officers beside the young and sturdy soldiers. "*And what do the American authorities say? Do they leave you alone?*" "*Officially, they don't, of course*", he answered with a nasty smile—"*but we behave discreetly, and generally they close their eyes*"

I made an effort to win his confidence and mentioned the name of some Cuban exiles, common friends that I had already met. Our conversation took on a very friendly tone. After an hour of conversation, he looked at his pals and said to me: "*I am going to tell you a secret that we have never told anyone before*". Then he stood up, while his associates did likewise, and asked me to follow him. We walked through a long passage into a large hall: "*This is the operations headquarters*" In the middle of the room, lying on a large table, there was a huge map of Cuba in relief. The map must have been six meters in length and three wide. Everywhere, mainly on the coast, there were little different colored flags. "*These are to differentiate the nature of the operations: sabotage, attacks against barracks, destruction of production centers, executions of Castro's agents, etc*". There were so many flags that, in comparison, the Normandy landings on 6th June 1944 seemed like a picnic. Considering the density, one might wonder how the Cuban regime could have resisted such an amount of attacks.

Nazario gave an order, and three smart youngsters dressed in military camouflage came in. They were part of the special force commandos. The one who seemed to be the chief, with the open gaze and nice smile, was Nazario's son or nephew: "*Allow me to present you*", he said," *the Alpha 66 men coming from the latest action in Cuba. They've just arrived*". He then told them to talk to me about their mission. Leaning over the map, the young paramilitary described a point on the northern coast of Cuba, to the west of Holguin, where he said they had fulfilled several acts of sabotage. "*We pursue them constantly; there isn't one week that we don't send a commando. We cause them considerable economic and human loss".*

I left the Alpha 66 center at night. I was astonished by the self-assured calm and confidence of the terrorist group I had just visited. To murder, destroy and exterminate, for them, seemed to be perfectly justifiable actions. They were at war. And for them, their main purpose, the "liberation" of the island, vindicated sabotage, terrorist actions and death.

Their fanatic anti-communism provided them with a shield against any compassion. They were killers serving the USA, but they were seen as heroes that the motherland would one day honor. I wonder to what extent I had been the object of attempted deception. Everything seemed very strange to me. Why did Nazario show me the secret headquarters that they don't allow anyone to see? And those commandos, that appeared by chance, coming from secret operations in Cuba? That reminded me of the famous ruse used in 1957 by Fidel Castro. When the *New York Times* journalist Herbert Mathew visited him in Sierra Maestra, he made him believe, ingeniously, that he had hundreds of guerrilla fighters and thousands of weapons, when he was only surrounded by a handful of men and a few guns.

What Herbert Mathew published on the front page of the New York Times gave huge prominence to the Cuban struggle and made its leader a world celebrity. I decided not to play that game in my report. (It was published in an issue of *Le Monde Diplomatique*, December 1981)

Some days later, I had an appointment with Luis Crespo, head of the Movimiento Insurreccional Martiano (MIM), another armed anti-Castro organization. My friends had advised me. "*That one is a real murderer*", they told me, '"*and he is an obsessive bomber who was the victim of his own deadly actions. He lost one eye, an arm, and a leg.* They believed he would prepare an ambush for me. *"Don't trust him, that guy must already know who you are. He can shoot you in the head and pretend that you entered his residence to rob. Don't go on your own".* Finally, they scared me so much that we agreed that I would enter on my own, but they would follow me and go for help if I didn't come out within two hours.

To add a bit of dramatic atmosphere, the meeting took place at dusk in Crespo's residence in a distant and lonely neighborhood. I was so nervous that I hit the car parked behind me and broke the rear lights of my rented vehicle.

Luis Crespo was waiting for me at the gate of his house, standing on the top step of the porch of his suburban home. He is of average height, and gives a very strange impression with that dead eye, stiff arm and his artificial leg. He had observed my disastrous maneuver and his first words were to explain how to cheat the insurance: "*Pick up all the pieces of glass"*, he said to me. "*Go to a parking area in a supermarket; park your car in an empty place, put the pieces of glass on the ground as if someone has just broken the lights, call the police and wait. Then say that another car collided with yours, but left without telling you his address. They will make a report. With that report you don't have to pay the rental insurance."*

I said to myself while listening to him, that if he had any intention of killing me, he would not have wasted his time explaining such a trick to me. That was really very clever on his part. He has the appearance of a "tough guy" or "bully". There was nothing friendly in his personality. He was alone. We introduced ourselves and the interview began. Luis Crespo explained to me that the Movimiento Insurreccional Martiano was founded in 1974 by Hector Alfonso Ruiz, also known as Hector Fabian. It had recently divided into two factions: one of them led by Ramon Saul Sanchez, also a member of the terrorist group Omega 7, and the other by Hector Fabian and himself.

Their group, he affirmed, was training to bring war to the

island. The commandos infiltrate the country regularly to commit sabotage and illegal offences. He laid claim to the ideas of José Marti, National Hero of the Cuban Independence. Crespo was planning to establish a real army composed of tens of thousands of Cubans that fought voluntarily with the Americans in the Viet Nam War, one thousand of them officers from the US Army reserve forces. According to him, there would be soon a huge popular revolt in Cuba.

Alpha 66 and MIM own important radio-stations in Florida which broadcast programs towards the island daily. The Alpha 66 station is managed by Diego Medina. They give instructions to the audience on how to use sabotage techniques in order to weaken the Cuban economy.

Those groups and others—like Abdala, Coordinación de las Organizaciones Revolucionarias Unidas, CORU (Coordination of United Revolutionary Organizations), the Poder Cubano (Cuban Power), Movimiento Nacionalista Cubano (Nationalist Cuban Movement), Frente de Liberación Nacional de Cuba (National Liberation Front of Cuba), are all inspired by a real militant myth. They are not interested in domestic policy, or even in the integration of their fellow citizens into the country that gives them shelter. They consider themselves temporary exiles and hardly feel solidarity towards other Latin groups settled in the United States. In other times, Alpha 66 and the MIM trained anti-Sandinista exiles in their camps.

Now, I think of those terrorists that I met in Miami, sheltered, financed and encouraged by the American authorities. I think about their criminal activities and of those more than two thousand Cuban victims of the odious terrorist actions coming from Florida. And I also think of the 5 anti terrorist fighters: Antonio Guerrero Rodriguez, Fernando Gonzalez Llort, Gerardo Fernadez Nordelo, Ramón Labañino Zalazar and René González Sehwerert, all of them condemned unjustly to inhumane sentences for infiltrating terrorist groups at the risk of their own lives. They tried to stop many crimes against innocent people. Their imprisonment is one of the biggest legal scandals of the beginning of the XXI Century.

CHAPTER SEVEN

SALIM LAMRANI

Salim Lamrani is a researcher at the Sorbonne University of Paris and is specialized in U.S.-Cuban relations since 1959.

He has published *Cuba Face à l'Empire: Propagande, guerre économique et terrorisme d'Etat* (Foreword by Noam Chomsky).

He regularly writes articles published in French, English, Spanish, German and Portuguese on U.S.-Cuban relations in newspapers and magazines all around the world.

The Cuban American National Foundation and International Terrorism

The brutality of American resentment towards the independence of Cuba is without historical equivalent and constitutes the key to the relations between the two nations, particularly since the triumph of the Revolution in 1959. Cuba is the country which has suffered the longest terrorist campaign in history. For ideological reasons, orthodox and conventional historiographers as well as the Western media consortia do not wish to recognize this truism, whereas the factual base is rich and undeniable. It is from the starting-point of this reality that it is advisable to analyze the role of the most influential Cuban lobby of the United States: the Cuban American National Foundation (CANF), its links with international terrorism and the impunity which it enjoys thanks to the U.S. authorities.

Birth of the Cuban American National Foundation

Along with the Bush II administration, the government of the late Ronald Reagan was the most aggressive in its foreign policies towards Cuba. Indeed, the majority of the members of the government of Mr. George W. Bush are recycled Reaganites, such as Donald Rumsfeld and John Negroponte. Unlike his predecessor, Jimmy Carter, who had been characterized by his attempts at rapprochement with the Cuban authorities and who had made it possible to renew bilateral relations between the two countries broken off since January 1961, Reagan decided to choose a policy of violence and threat. Furthermore, his advisers had "to dissuade him from his private fantasy that Cuba could be *liberated* by the force of the weapons".[1]

The Santa Fe Document, established by the hawks of the Republican radical rightwing, which recommended the utmost inflexibility towards the government of Havana, became the guiding principle for Latin-American affairs. In Reagan's logic of overthrowing the Cuban government, Roger Fontaine, one of the ideologues of the Santa Fe group, proposed the creation of an autonomous entity able to put pressure on a Congress reluctant to follow the warmongering strategy of the administration of the day. Richard Allen, Reagan's adviser on National Security, gathered a group of Cuban millionaires who represented the most recalcitrant part of Batista's extreme rightwing. They had already proved their allegiance towards the United States and had a common enemy: the Cuban Revolution.[2]

It was within this framework of renewal of the Cold War, where the military approach to international affairs took a step towards becoming conventional diplomacy, that, following a directive of President Ronald Reagan's National Security Council, CANF was born in 1981. It is the intellectual creation of the director of the CIA, William Casey, considered the most influential director of the agency since Allen Dulles. CANF met the needs of Reagan's ultra-reactionary policy towards Cuba and was intended to serve the imperialist interests of Washington.[3]

Created on the model of *American Israel Public Affairs Committee*, the most powerful lobby of the United States, its role consisted of hyping up the issues and lobbying Congress and public opinion. It was necessary, according to a secret and now declassified document of the National Security Council (U.S. Policy in Exchange America and Cuba through F.Y. ' 84, Summary Paper), to avoid "the proliferation of states [like] Cuba". The CANF was supposed to launch a campaign in favor of human rights in Cuba, denounce the government of Havana by means of an international propaganda campaign, in order to increase economic sanctions and all types of aggression against the Cuban population, and "to prevent any negotiation led by Congress".[4]

The president chosen to direct the new structure was Jorge Mas Canosa. He "was the worst element of the Cuban community of the United States", according to the former U.S. Attorney General, Ramsey Clark.[5] A former CIA agent and a mercenary during the of Bay of Pigs invasion, Jorge Mas Canosa had succeeded in making a fortune with a public sector construction firm. Thus, the alliance between U.S. interests and the old former political and economic elites of Batista's dictatorship allowed the creation of what was going to become the pre-eminent Cuban lobby of the United States.[6]

Effective lobbying

From the moment of its creation, CANF was given the responsibility for reducing to ashes the attempts at rapprochement between Washington and Havana outlined under the government of Mr. Carter. This government had accepted the installation of a U.S. diplomatic presence in Havana (SINA) and a Cuban one in

Washington. It had also successfully started negotiations concerning questions of emigration, the resumption of flights between the two countries and the release of "political prisoners".

Radio and TV Martí

In September 13, 1985, CANF succeeded in persuading the Congress to vote in favor of the Radio Martí project. This radio broadcasting project, equipped with an initial budget of 6 million dollars and entirely financed by the U.S. taxpayer, was intended to transmit propaganda programs about the Island. After having been refused at first by Congress in 1982, President Reagan secretly ordered its implementation as of May 1985, with a 14-hour daily program. The propaganda focus of Radio Martí was so obvious that a member of the Congress, opposed to the legislation, proposed to call it "John Foster Dulles Cold War Mentality Memorial Radio Broadcasting to Cuba Act".[7]

In 2004, Radio Martí employed 108 people and had a budget of 15 million dollars. Its programs encourage subversion, actions of sabotage and the creation of a situation of chaos. In short, any action likely to create sufficient disorder to lead to the fall of the Cuban government is virulently preached. The work of Radio Martí also consists in inhibiting any attempt at normalizing the relations between Cuba and the United States. The Cuban lobby in Florida is the only one which has such a tool in its political war against the government of Havana.[8]

The transmissions of Radio Martí violate the national Cuban air-waves and the sovereignty of the nation. However, the hoped-for effects of the installation of this transmitter are not satisfactory, thanks to the effective jamming carried out by the Cuban authorities. At the time of the creation of Radio operator Martí, Havana had however proposed a deal to Washington: Cuba would not scramble the waves of the aforementioned station provided that the United States made it possible for Havana to broadcast on their territory. The offer was obviously rejected.

Several corruption scandals broke out within the personnel section and the editorial team. A report written in June 1999 by Voice of America (VOA) on the functioning of Radio Martí noted that "questionable programs had been broadcast" and that "the credibility of the news broadcasts and the professionalism" of the radio broadcasting chain appeared defective. Certain programs "breached the broadcasting standards of VOA" by their "lack of balance, impartiality and objectivity and adequate sources [of information]". Besides the "very lax editorial control ", programs contained "obscene and vulgar references", in breach of the applicable legislation. The conclusion of the report was that the "lack of expertise and professionalism" strongly affected the charter of Voice of America, as well as the objectives of U.S. foreign policy.[9]

However, the power of the CANF set aside the tarnished record of Radio Martí, to obtain, through political cunning, the creation of the television channel, TV Martí, on March 27, 1990. This had the same prerogatives as Radio Martí and was at the privileged disposal of the Cuban extremists. Its effectiveness was called into question by the Republican representative of Arizona, Mr. Jeff Flake: "We have Radio and TV Marti and Congress spends 26 million dollars for the two bodies. And well, after 12 years and 10 million dollars per annum for TV Marti, there is not one piece of proof showing that the Cubans saw one minute of it and we continue to produce it" at the expense of the American taxpayer.[10]

The Torricelli and Helms-Burton Acts and the new wave of economic strangulation

CANF's enormous capacity for political coercion was also illustrated in 1992, with the passing of the Torricelli Act, and more particularly in 1996, with the approval of the Helms-Burton Act. The upsurge of the economic sanctions, just after the collapse of the Soviet bloc in 1991, clearly showed that the political rhetoric of the various U.S. administrations concerning the "red peril" was only a smoke screen intended to hide hegemonic intentions with regard to Cuba. Indeed, if the diplomatic rhetoric of the Cold war had a credibility anywhere above zero, the United States would have immediately standardized its relations with the Havana government at the time of "the end of history". But on the contrary, George H. Bush in 1992 and Bill Clinton in 1996 made the economic strangulation of the Cuban people an absolute priority.[11]

On May 6, 2004, under pressure from CANF, President Bush made public an impressive 454-page report entitled "Commission for Assistance to a Free Cuba". Written by the Secretary of State, Colin L. Powell, it is actually the intellectual creation of Otto Reich, a notorious friend of CANF and spokesman for the most backward-looking fringe of the Cuban exile. The document in question imposes severe measures which hurt the Cuban population of the Island, already a serious victim of the economic sanctions imposed by Washington since 1960, as well as the Cuban-American community which sees its rights severely cut back. A few months from the presidential elections, the U.S. president wanted to attract the favors of Florida and its strong anti-revolutionary electorate.[12]

Washington has woven a network of legislation against Cuba without historical precedent which violates the highest International Conventions, among them, the Convention for the

Prevention and Repression of the Crime of Genocide, approved on December 9, 1948 and ratified by the government of the United States. The aforesaid convention bans "the intentional subjection of a group to living conditions likely to lead to its complete or partial destruction". Economic sanctions have cost Cuba more than 70 billion dollars and have been condemned by the United Nations, the European Union, the Organization of the American States, the Inter-American Legal Committee, the Inter-American Commission on Human Rights, the World Trade Organization and other international bodies. CANF has a substantial responsibility in the maintenance and the reinforcement of this economic punishment.[13]

International terrorism as a means of political expression

In addition to its political work amongst the members of Congress, one of the characteristics of the CANF is its recourse to terrorist violence as an instrument of ideological expression. Enjoying a perfect impunity with the U.S. authorities, this extremist body did not hesitate to resort to para-military methods in its declared war against Cuba and its inhabitants. Luis Posada Carriles, mercenary and former CIA agent, originator of several dozens of bloody attacks against Cuba, is an old friend "of the Latin-American terrorist network".[14] Trained at the regrettably well-known School of the Americas at Fort Benning in Georgia, he took part particularly in the military aggression at the Bay of Pigs in April 1961. After this crushing failure, he devoted his life to violence and terrorism against Cuba, while all the time serving U.S. interests.[15]

Targeting the civilians

It is important to point out the most atrocious crimes that Posada Carriles carried out with the support of the United States and the Cuban extreme right wing. October 6, 1976 is a date without precedent, which, if Western society were intellectually free, would be known to all, especially after September 11, 2001. For the first time in history, air terrorism was used as a means of political expression. A Cuban commercial aircraft, coming from Barbados, exploded in mid air. Seventy-three people lost their lives, among them the Cuban Junior fencing team, made up of 24 people, which had just won the Pan-American games. The investigation carried out by the government of Barbados discovered links between the terrorists and members of the U.S. embassy on the Island.[16]

After a short stay in a Venezuelan prison, Posada Carriles succeeded in escaping thanks to his connections with the CIA, the State Department and CANF, which provided 26 000 dollars to bribe the guards. Thereafter, Posada Carriles took up residence in Central America and offered his services to Colonel Oliver North, seriously implicated in the terrorist war against the Sandinista government of Nicaragua.[17]

Attacks against tourist structures

In 1997, several bombs exploded in various tourist centers of Havana, resulting in the death of Fabio di Celmo, a young Italian holiday-maker. The investigations of the Cuban authorities led to the arrest of the culprit, a Salvadorian recruited, trained and financed by Luis Posada Carriles. At the time of the lawsuit, he revealed its links with members of the extreme Cuban rightwing in Florida and his intention of targeting the tourist infrastructures, in order to affect this vital sector of the Cuban economy. The danger undergone by innocent people was of secondary importance, not to be taken into consideration. For the enemies of the Cuban population, the end justifies the means.[18]

During an interview, published in the *New York Times* on July 12, 1998, Posada Carriles acknowledged that he was financed by CANF. After praising himself as being the person who had made the greatest number of attacks against Cuba, he announced that he was paid by the former president of CANF, Jorge Mas Canosa. "Jorge controlled everything" he declared "each time that I needed money, he asked someone to send me 5 000 dollars, 10 000 dollars, 15 000 dollars". At the time of each financial transaction, the following message was attached: "This is for the church".[19]

All in all, Mas Canosa, CANF and, more particularly, Feliciano Foyo, the treasurer of the Foundation, provided more than 200 000 dollars to one of the worst terrorists in the world. Posada Carriles boasted about being the paramilitary wing of CANF and added: "As you can see, the FBI and the CIA do not bother me, and I am neutral with them. Each time I can give them a hand, I do so". He also revealed that he knew "a very highly placed person" in the government who protected him.[20]

Concerning the death of the Italian tourist, Posada Carriles simply restricted himself to noting that "this Italian was in the wrong place at the wrong time". As regards problems of conscience, he answered the journalists clearly: "I sleep like a baby". He finished the interview by admitting that he had at least four passports, including a U.S. one, and that he went to Miami whenever he wanted to. Following this declaration, no legal proceedings were taken against this individual.[21]

According to the *New York Times*, the FBI was aware of the terrorist campaign that the Cuban extremists had planned against the hotel industry, but they did not take any measures to stop the culprits or to inform the Cuban government. The reason?

Informing the Cuban authorities that a wave of terrorist attacks was on the point of being started on their territory was against the national interest of the United States. The fight against terrorism is not the priority of the U.S government, which harbors and protects many authors of attacks. Only those who do not defend its political agenda are hunted down.[22]

In March 1999, Percy Francisco Alvarado, a Guatemalan agent of Cuban National Security, having infiltrated the Cuban American National Foundation, made a statement at the time of the court case against the assassin of Mr. Di Celmo. He confirmed that he had received 20 000 dollars on behalf of Francisco "Pepe" Hernandez", the president of CANF, in order to explode two bombs in tourist areas of Havana. At the time of the hearing, it was declared that "the CANF played an active and hegemonic part in the financing and organization of the terrorist acts", by means of the creation of a secret paramilitary group bearing the name of *Cuban National Front* (CNF).[23]

Assassinating the Cuban president

Reinforced by his freedom of action and the support from CANF, Posada Carriles continued his activities. On November 17, 2000, he tried to assassinate the Cuban president while he spoke at a conference at the University of Panama. He had placed a 15 kilo bomb of C4 explosives in the university enclosure where 2 000 students had come to attend the speech by Fidel Castro. The Panamanian police force estimated that the explosion could have caused hundreds of victims. Arrested by the authorities of the country in question, Posada Carriles was judged and sentenced to eight years' imprisonment for terrorist activities.[24]

All attempts by the CANF to release Posada Carriles failed. These included political pressure, attempts at corruption and all kinds of threats towards the Panamanian legal authorities; but a new collection of funds was organized in Miami by the extreme Cuban right, in which Francisco "Pepe" Hernández participated.[25]

However, an incredible event occurred on August 25, 2004. Mireya Moscoso, President of Panama, pardoned the four dangerous individuals on August 25, 2004, thus causing the severing of diplomatic relations between Cuba and Panama.[26] At once condemned by the future president of Panama, Martin Torrijos, the decision caused an outcry among public opinion in the country. Julia E. Sweig, a Cuba expert at the Council on Foreign Relations, was very explicit: "This reeks of political and diplomatic cronyism" she underlined, referring to the links between Mr. Jeb Bush, the brother of the U.S. President, and Mrs. Moscoso.[27]

The Cuban-American National Foundation (CANF) was pleased with the release of the four terrorists, at least one of whom, Luis Posada Carriles, was financed by its former president Jorge Mas Canosa as chief of its paramilitary wing.[28] Francisco "Pepe" Hernandez was delighted by the decision of Mireya Moscoso. "This is a victory for all exiles and a triumph of justice, beyond the strategy chosen to bring democracy to Cuba," he said.[29]

Francisco Hernandez is also implicated in at least one assassination attempt against Fidel Castro. In October 1997, U.S. coastguards in the territorial waters of Puerto Rico, thinking that they were dealing with drug traffickers, stopped a high-speed motorboat heading for the Venezuelan Island, Marguerite. After having hailed it, they discovered that the four people on board had a whole military arsenal at their disposal, composed of assault rifles with telescopic sights worth 7 000 dollars, a satellite telephone, a great deal of ammunition and military uniforms.

The four individuals (three of whom collaborated closely with the Foundation), accustomed to four decades of impunity, did not hesitate to announce their intentions openly to the coastguards: "These weapons are intended to assassinate Fidel

Castro," said one of them. Angel Alfonso Alemán then 57 years old, Francisco Córdova, 50, Angel M. Hernández Rojo, 64, Juan Bautista Márquez, 61, made up this strange terrorist group. The investigation carried out by Hector Pesquera, chief of the FBI in Puerto Rico showed that one of the two rifles belonged to Francisco "Pepe" Hernández and that the yacht was the property of José Antonio "Toñín" Llama, a member of the executive Committee of the CANF. But the special agent voiced reservations, detecting the political aspect of the problem. In spite of the gravity of the charges, "it may be that there are implications in the area of foreign policy" he admitted. Both leaders of the Foundation escaped legal proceedings thanks to their status.[30]

In January 1998, Juan Bautista Márquez, released on bail, was again stopped by the Drug Enforcement Agency for importing 365 kilos of cocaine, for money laundering and plotting drug trafficking. The charges against him (conspiracy to commit assassination and drug trafficking) were very serious and he could not avoid several years of loss of liberty. But this was without taking into account the powerful pressure machine of the CANF which, like a steamroller, had been set in motion. All legal proceedings were abandoned for reasons which will remain in the annals of infamy. For example, the lawyer of defendant Angel Alfonso Alemán, was Ricardo Pesquera, the cousin of... Hector Pesquera, the FBI agent in charge of the affair. Not a single one of the four terrorists was inconvenienced. To this day they continue their conspiracies to destroy the Cuban Revolution and even boast, in various media, of being above the law. As for officer Pesquera, he was named chief of the FBI in Miami and played an important part in the arrest of the five Cuban agents who had infiltrated the terrorist groups.[31]

The newspaper *New Times* of Miami questioned CANF concerning the terrorist attacks against Cuba. They gave had the following answer: "We do not condemn a person who tries to end the conditions which oppress his people, his family and himself". These people have the right "to fight for their freedom" according to the organization, it does not matter if children, women or elderly people perish in the attacks.[32]

In 1998, Mr. Robert Sheer of the *Los Angeles Times* wrote: "For almost 40 years, we isolated Cuba because of the idea that this small island was a center of terrorism in the hemisphere, and year after year, we have new evidence that in fact the United States terrorized Cuba and not the opposite".[33]

Furthermore, a federal prosecutor confirmed that "for a long time", work was carried out "to collect information and to demobilize" the extremist groups, "to dismantle them rather than to stop them". He acknowledged that "the policy is designed to protect the informant and to avoid lawsuits which have little chance of succeeding because of the sympathy of the jury towards anti-Castro exiles" who practice terrorist violence, "and because of the weakness of the laws of the United States prohibiting acts of violence against foreign governments".[34]

The Case of the Five

Contrary to a generally accepted idea, international terrorism has never been the means of expression of the weak. It is above all the political weapon of the powerful and this obvious fact would be known of all if there was any kind of leaning towards the truth. Since 1959, that is to say, since the birth of Cuba as an independent and sovereign nation, the United States has based its relations with Cuba on coercive violence, whose first victim was the population of the Island. Thus, the use of brutality against the Caribbean Archipelago was set up as an unshakable doctrine by successive U.S. administrations. This established fact is corroborated by the iniquitous treatment reserved for the Five.

The trial of the five Cubans—Gerardo Hernández Nordelo,

Ramón Labañino Salazar, Antonio Guerrero Rodríguez, Fernando González Llort and Rene González Sehweret—who infiltrated the fascistic par-military groups of Florida, such as *Brothers to the Rescue*, *Alpha 66* and *Movimiento Democracia* (whose members have a long experience in international terrorism) in order to neutralize them, is a good illustration. The Five succeeded in preventing at least a hundred and seventy attacks against Cuba, by alerting the authorities in Havana in time. The Cuban government then informed its U.S. counterpart and, in June 1998, a delegation of the FBI went to Cuba where they received full documentation concerning the intrigues of the extremists of Miami. After having received this information and evidence of the illegal and dangerous activities of the aforesaid groups from the Cuban authorities, the FBI, instead of tackling the criminals in question, arrested the informants who, at the risk of their lives, had infiltrated these fascist groups.[35]

The penal procedure was nothing less than a grotesque parody. To cite just one example among so many others: the defense did not have access to the evidence put forward by the prosecutor because it was mysteriously classified as secret. The affair was so stained by irregularities that the *International Association of Democratic Lawyers*, which has members in more than ninety countries, the *National Jury Project* and the *National Lawyers Guild* requested a retrial in vain. 31 members of the British Parliament also condemned the trial. Among the legislative violations was that of the 6th Amendment of the U.S. Constitution which establishes the right of the defendant to a regular trial and an impartial jury, two conditions which do not exist in Miami. The deeply politicized atmosphere in Florida and the specious press campaign launched against the Five before the beginning of the legal process, condemned them unambiguously, making them the perfect scapegoats of an anti-revolutionary hostility set up as a dogma for more than four decades.[36]

The testimonies of General Whilhem, ex-Commander-in-Chief of the intelligence services; of Admiral Eugene Carroll, ex-chief assistant of naval operations and Colonel George Bucker, member of the U.S. Air Defense Command, attested to the legitimacy of the activities of the five defendants by underlining the danger represented by the heirs of Batista. General James Clapper, ex director of the DIA (Defense Intelligence Agency—the secret services of the Pentagon), who appeared as an expert before the Court, affirmed that the defendants had not taken actions concerned with espionnage.[37]

The Five faced 26 criminal charges including "conspiracy and fraud against the government" of the United States, and "the sending of information concerning defense affairs to a foreign government", in other words espionage. They were all found guilty of all the main indictments and were condemned to extremely severe prison sentences.[38]

This affair reveals a lot about the role and the impunity of the Cuban terrorist groups of Florida. From a legal point of view, espionage consists of revealing the secrets of foreign or enemy powers, and thus can be carried out only against bodies belonging to a government. However, the Five infiltrated non-governmental organizations which were seriously involved in international terrorism. Thus, U.S. authorities implicitly admit that they consider the anti-Cuban terrorists as allies in their struggle against the government of Havana. This avowal clearly shows that the fight against terrorism was never the priority of the United States since they protect associations which preach violence and use it indiscriminately.

Thus, providing information relating to the intrigues of counterrevolutionary extremist groups means "damaging the national security" of the United States as if they were an integral part of the government. This admission is not surprising if any attention is given to U.S. foreign policy towards Cuba since 1959.

All means were used to assassinate the Cuban Revolution: direct military invasion, terrorist attacks and economic, bacteriological, political and diplomatic warfare. Such a confession just shows a little more the lies of the so-called war against terrorism which is actually only a specious front intended to disguise imperialist hegemony.

Condoleeza Rice, ex-President Bush's National Security adviser and now Secretary of State, has referred to the "intolerable case of Cuba", and this reflection is not devoid of justification if looked at from the point of view of U.S. political strategists.[39] Indeed it is "intolerable" that a country of the Third World which is, in addition, in the back-yard of the United States, dares to defy the Masters of the world by reserving its natural resources for its people and not for the economic and financial interests of Washington. It is inadmissible that a nation asphyxiated by a legislative network of sanctions which even a European power would have difficulty in tolerating, can still resist after more than 45 years of economic strangulation; and worse still, "social policy is unquestionably one area in which Cuba has excelled by guaranteeing an equitable distribution of income and well-being of the population, while investing in human capital", according to the report published by the United Nations Economic Commission on Latin America (ECLA).[40] And the United States cannot tolerate this heresy, hence this policy of institutionalized terror.

If Cuba yields to the orders of Washington, if it agrees to give up its sovereignty, and to subject its resources to the voracious appetites of the multinationals, it will be regarded as an integral part of the "democratic" world and will escape from paramilitary violence. But as long as it has not met these conditions, it will continue to be the privileged target of the attacks of Washington and terrorism coming from Florida. As the Cuban Apostle José Martí, hero of the second War of Independence said: "Freedom is very expensive, and it is necessary either to resign oneself to live without it, or to decide to pay the price". And the Cubans have made their choice.

As long as Cuba continues to defy the dominant and dogmatic market ideology while showing, by its example, that it is possible to be released from the desolation of underdevelopment, not by applying the diktats of the International Monetary Fund (IMF) and the World Bank, but by placing the human being at the centre of its social project, it will always be the target of para-military attacks orchestrated from the United States. As long as it refuses to apply the discipline of market and profit, U.S. terrorism will not cease.

The roots of U.S. hostility do not go back to 1959 but to the beginning of the 19th century; for American expansionism always wanted to monopolize the Island. In 1902, an American bookshop circulated a map of Cuba under the title: "Our New Colony: Cuba".[41] The United States will do all that is in its capacity to return to this pre-revolutionary situation, to make of Cuba another Puerto Rico, another Haiti or another Dominican Republic—where the opulence of a minority contrasts with the indigence of the majority and where U.S. transnationals make astronomical profits, and it will restlessly cling to the same voluble and obsolete rhetoric which it recycles endlessly.

During the 19th century, while he was fighting against Spanish tyranny, José Martí wrote: " There are two paths for people when they are born: The path of slavery, which crushes and subjugates; and the path of the star, which illuminates but kills. You will choose the star. Your path will be hard and it will be marked with blood. But wherever a single person falls in the name of justice, thousands more will rise up. And when there are no more people, then the stones will rise up." Gerardo, Ramon, Antonio, Fernando and Rene, at their birth people see two paths opening up before them. You have chosen the star.

PART B

THE STORY OF THE CUBAN FIVE

CHAPTER EIGHT

LEONARD WEINGLASS

Leonard Weinglass has been involved in liberal and radical causes since his graduation from Yale Law School in 1958. He has been co-chair of the left-leaning National Lawyer's Guild. He has represented Pentagon Papers defendant Anthony Russo, Angela Davis, Jane Fonda, Mumia Abu Jamal, Bill and Emily Harris of the Symbionese Liberation Army (the group charged with the kidnapping of Patricia Hearst), and Amy Carter, daughter of President Jimmy Carter, who in 1987 was charged with seizing a University of Massachusetts building in protest of on-campus recruitment by the CIA. Weinglass has also traveled extensively to world trouble spots and to the sites of trials of dissidents. Among the countries he has visited are Cuba, Vietnam, the West Bank, Iran (during the hostage crisis), El Salvador, Nicaragua, and China. He is currently representing the Cuban Five.

The Trial of the Cuban Five

Five Cuban men, later to become known as the Cuban Five, were arrested in Miami, Florida in September, 1998 and charged with 26 counts of violating the federal laws of the United States. 24 of those charges, being relatively minor and technical offenses, alleged the use of false names and failure to register as foreign agents. None of the charges claimed they used weapons, engaged in violence or destroyed property.

The Five had come to the United States from Cuba following years of violence perpetrated by armed mercenaries from the Cuban exile community in Florida. Cuba suffered significant casualties and property destruction. Cuban protests to the United

States government and the United Nations had fallen on deaf ears. Following the demise of the socialist states in the early 90's the violence escalated as Cuba struggled to establish a tourism industry. The Miami mercenaries responded with a violent campaign to dissuade foreigners from visiting. A bomb was found in the airport terminal in Havana, tourist buses were bombed, as were hotels (an Italian tourist was killed). Boats from Miami traveled to Cuba and shelled hotels and tourist facilities.

The mission of the Five was not to obtain U.S. military secrets, but rather to monitor the terrorist activities of the mercenaries and report back to Cuba. They were never armed, never sought to obtain security clearances, did not seek or obtain a single page of classified information, inflicted no injuries and did no property damage. Yet, three are serving life sentences in America's prisons and one is doing two life sentences.

The two main charges against them alleged a theory of prosecution that's ordinarily used in politically charged cases: conspiracy. A conspiracy is an illegal agreement between two or more persons to commit a crime. The crime need not occur. Once such an agreement is established, the crime is complete. All the prosecution need do is demonstrate through circumstantial evidence that there *must have been* an agreement. Rarely is there actual and direct proof of an illegal agreement unless one of the alleged actors turns state's evidence and testifies. In a political case, such as this one, juries often infer agreement, absent evidence of a crime, on the basis of the politics, minority status or national identity of the accused. This is precisely why and how the conspiracy charge was used here. In addition, each of the two conspiracy charges carries a sentence of life in prison.

The first conspiracy charge alleged that three of the Five had agreed to commit espionage. The government argued at the outset that it need not prove that espionage occurred, merely that there was an agreement to do it sometime in the future. While the media was quick to refer to the Five as spies, the legal fact, and actual truth, was that this was not a case of spying, but of an alleged agreement to do it. Thus relieved of the duty of proving actual espionage, the prosecutors set about convincing a Miami jury that these five Cuban men, living in their midst, *must have had* such an agreement.

The second conspiracy charge was added seven months after the first. It alleged that one of the Five, Gerardo Hernandez, conspired with others, non-indicted Cuban officials, to shoot down two aircraft flown by Cuban exiles from Miami as they entered, or were about to enter, Cuban airspace. They were intercepted by Cuban Migs, killing all four aboard. Hernandez, who had successfully infiltrated the group that sent the aircraft, was not charged with tipping off the Cubans about the planned flight, its route or mission, but rather with being part of a conspiracy to shoot down the aircraft because he was warned beforehand not to fly, or to let his comrades fly, on those days. While the government attorneys argued to the Court of Appeals that the trial judge's proposed instruction on that charge made conviction virtually impossible, the Miami jury nonetheless quickly convicted Gerardo.

The trial got underway in the late Fall of 2000. It ended seven months later, in June 2001, becoming the longest criminal trial in the United States during that time. Over 70 witnesses testified, more than 30 for the defense, including two retired generals, one retired admiral and a presidential advisor who served in the White House. The trial record consumed over 119 volumes of transcript. In addition there were 15 volumes of pre-trial testimony and argument. More than 800 exhibits were introduced into evidence, some as long as 40 pages. The record was massive.

The twelve jurors returned verdicts of guilty on all 26 counts in early June, 2001 without asking a single question or requesting a rereading of any testimony, unusual in a trial of this length and complexity.

The Judge then sentenced the Five to maximum sentences in December, 2001, while the U.S. was still reeling from 9/11, giving Gerardo Hernandez two life sentences, Antonio Guerrero and Ramon Labanino to life in prison, Fernando Gonzalez, to 19 years, and Renee Gonzalez, to 15 years.

The Five immediately appealed their convictions and sentences. Their appeal was to the Eleventh Circuit Court of Appeal, which sits in Atlanta, Georgia. A three-judge panel traveled to Miami to hear oral argument on the appeal on March 10, 2004, allocating just 15 minutes to the five lawyers who presented the Five. As of this writing in July, 2004, no decision has been made.

The Jury

As is the custom and practice in the United States, the government's evidence against the Five had to be submitted to a jury of 12 persons, drawn from the Miami community, who serve as the judges of the facts and render a decision. The law requires that the twelve be «fair and impartial.» If there is even a probability of unfairness because of prejudice in the community, the law requires that the case be transferred to a place where fair-minded jurors can be found.

In Miami, it took over a week of questioning no fewer than 168 people to find 12 who said they could be fair and neutral judges of agents of the Cuban government. However, even these twelve had fixed opinions that clearly tainted their judgment. The head of the jury, or foreman, told the court: «I believe Castro is a Communist dictator and I am opposed to Communism. I would like to see him gone and democracy established.» Similar comments were made by other jurors. Nonetheless the case remained in Miami.

As one of the Five, Antonio Guerrero, told the Court at the time of his sentencing: «When it comes to Cuba, Miami is an impossible place for justice,» By that time, the defense had filed no less than five motions to move the trial to a more neutral site. It was obvious that Miami was the last place in the world the five Cubans could get a fair trial. Social science backs up Guerrero's observation. One of the nation's foremost experts in the Cuban exile phenomenon, Dr. Lisandro Pérez[34], wrote, «the possibility of selecting twelve citizens of Miami-Dade County who can be impartial in a case involving acknowledged agents of the Cuban government is virtually zero.»

In no other district would the defendants face prospective jurors, at least 20% of whom were men and women who had left Cuba because they disagreed with the government which the defendants were trying to protect. Among those reporting for jury service was a director of the extreme right-wing Cuban-American National Foundation, which provided funding for the flights into Cuban airspace, as well as more obviously terroristic ventures. He was eliminated only because of what even the judge characterized as his «bizarre behavior.» In no other jurisdiction would the accused face at least sixteen prospective jurors who personally knew someone identified as a victim of the shootdown, or a family member.

Miami stands alone as the only city in the United States where Cuban musicians cannot perform and Cuban artists cannot display their art without meeting riotous protest. Organizers of academic conferences require special protection if Cuban academics will be attending. Miami is the only city in the United States that would prefer to cancel international sporting events to having Cuban athletes compete. Even the prestigious Latin Grammy music awards had to be transferred out of Miami twice because of violence. Attitudes toward anyone perceived as being friendly towards Cuba are so hostile that one of the prospective jurors readily admitted that he would be afraid of retaliation «*if I didn't come back with a verdict in agreement with what the Cuban community feels, how they feel the verdict should be.»*

It was in such a setting that the case of the Five proceeded to trial.

The Evidence

A. On the charge of Conspiracy to Commit Espionage

In his opening statement to the jury, the prosecutor conceded that the Five did not have in their possession a single page of classified government information even though the government had succeeded in obtaining over 20,000 pages of correspondence between them and Cuba. Moreover, that correspondence was reviewed by one of the highest-ranking military officers in the Pentagon on intelligence (the Director of Defense Intelligence, a three star general) who, when asked, acknowledged that he couldn't recall seeing any national defense information. The law requires the presence of national defense information in order to prove the crime of espionage.

Rather, all the prosecution relied upon was the fact that one of the Five, Antonio Guerrero, worked in a metal shop on the Boca Chica Navy training base in Southern Florida. The base was completely open to the public, and even had a special viewing area set aside to allow people to take photographs of planes on the runways. While working there Guerrero had never applied for a security clearance, had no access to restricted areas, and had never tried to enter any. Despite intense intimidation from the prosecution, some fellow-workers testified that he was an ordinary, hard-working, out-going person who showed no particular interest in secure areas. Indeed, while the FBI had him under surveillance for two years before the arrests, there was no testimony from any of the agents about a single act of wrongdoing on his part.

Far from providing damning evidence for the prosecution, the documents seized from the defendants were used by the defense because they demonstrated the non-criminal nature of Guerrero's activity at the base. He was to «discover and report in a timely manner the information or indications that denote the preparation of a military aggression against Cuba» on the basis of «what he could see» by observing «open public activities.» This included information visible to any member of the public: the comings and goings of aircraft. He was also cutting news articles out of the local paper which reported on the military units stationed there.

Former high-ranking US military and security officials testified that Cuba presents no military threat to the United States, that there is no useful military information to be obtained from Boca Chica, and that Cuba's interest in obtaining the kind of information presented at trial was «to find out whether indeed we are preparing to attack them» (Major General Edward Breed Atkeson (US Army, instructor at US Defense Intelligence College).

Information that is generally available to the public cannot form the basis of an espionage prosecution. Once again, General Clapper, when asked, «would you agree that open source intelligence is not espionage?» replied, «that is correct.» So lacking in convincing evidence of espionage was the prosecution's case that after all the evidence had been presented, it was compelled to argue to the jury that they should convict merely if they believed there was an agreement to commit espionage at some unspecified time in the future. Nonetheless, after hearing the prosecution's highly improper argument, repeated 3 times, that the five Cubans were in this country «for the purpose of destroying the United States,» the jury, more swayed by passion than the law and evidence, convicted.

B. On the charge of Conspiracy to Commit Murder against Gerardo Hernandez

This charge was based on the February 24, 1996 shootdown of 2 aircraft by the Cuban air force which had taken off from Florida and headed for Cuba with the clear intent of penetrating its airspace, if not already in it. The facts presented at trial made it obvious that Hernández was not responsible for the fate of the men in the planes, their death was not the result of any premeditated murder, and there was no agreement that if the planes were downed, it should be in international, rather than Cuban airspace, as the law requires. All three are required for conviction.

The evidence showed that on February 24, 1996, in what was by then a familiar scenario, Cuban exiles took off from Florida in 3 planes and, once airborne, veered off their flight plans and headed straight for Cuba. After being warned by Cuban air control that they were entering a prohibited area, they were intercepted, and two were shot down by the Cuban Air Force. Four Miami residents died. In a recording played at trial, the pilot of one of the planes could be heard laughing as the planes deliberately violated the order to turn back. Prosecutors used the law of conspiracy to argue that Hernández, who had infiltrated groups such as Brothers to the Rescue (who sponsored this flight), was alerting Cuba of its plans to inflict terror and possibly bomb Cuba, and was therefore responsible for murder.

It is not a crime for Cuba to shoot down aircraft flying over its own territorial waters or land. Thus, the trial judge ruled that in order to convict Hernández of this charge, the prosecution would have to prove that before the planes even took off, he was part of a specific plan or agreement to down them before they reached Cuban territory. Otherwise, the United States would have no power to try anyone because the prosecution could not prove that there was an agreement that critical events were to take place in what the United States claims as its «special maritime or territorial jurisdiction.»

The prosecution conceded that it had no evidence whatsoever regarding any agreement about where the intruding planes might be stopped. It thus filed an extraordinary appeal to the Court of Appeals for the 11th Circuit, complaining that, given the evidence presented at trial, the ruling created an «insurmountable obstacle» for conviction. The appeal was rejected, and the jury was instructed that it must find beyond a reasonable doubt that there was a specific agreement to shoot down the planes in international waters. The jury hardly noticed the «insurmountable obstacle», and convicted in record time.

C. The 24 other charges

Most of these charges related to the Five creating and using false identities (two of the Five, Antonio Guerrero and Renee Gonzalez were U.S. citizens and traveled and lived under their lawful names). That these minor charges were technically violated was not denied by the Five. Rather, they argued an established defense allowed under U.S. law: the defense of necessity or justification. That defense provides that one may violate a law (usually technical in nature and one that doesn't involve personal injury or property damage) if the motivation for the violation is to prevent a greater harm, such as bodily injury or property damage. Thus, one may legally trespass onto a neighbor's property, a technical violation, in order to put out a fire. Certainly, using false identities to prevent terror attacks on one's countrymen would appear to qualify for the defense.

Over 35 documents and a number of witnesses were presented by the defense to establish that Cuba had suffered deaths, injury and property damage at the hands of the groups that had been infiltrated by the Five. Even the Court, in sentencing two of the Five, referred to these groups as «terrorist» groups. Nonetheless, the Court refused to allow the jury to consider the defense of necessity or justification, and three of the Five were convicted of all the false identity charges.

The remaining charges, again technical in nature, alleged that the Five failed to register with the Attorney General of the United States as «foreign agents» as the law requires. Here, also, the defense of necessity or justification should have been applied. But, once again, the Court refused to allow the jury to consider this defense. All Five were convicted on those counts as well.

Other Aspects of the Case

A. CONDITIONS OF CONFINEMENT

For 17 months prior to their trial, and while they were still presumed innocent, the Five were confined in punishment, isolation cells in an effort to coerce them into pleading guilty. These cells are ordinarily reserved only for convicted felons who misbehave in prison. They never wavered, but the ability to prepare their defense was impaired.

B. FISA AND CIPA

Agents of the U.S. government committed five break-ins of the apartments of the Five prior to their arrest in an effort to illegally gather the evidence to be used against them. Those break-ins were allowed by a secret court, The Foreign Intelligence Surveillance Court, under a law know as FISA, which allows violations of the protections of the U.S. Constitution and is condemned by civil libertarians.

Then, operating under another controversial law, called CIPA, or Classified Information Procedure Act, the government classified each of the documents they seized from the Five, refusing to turn some of them back to the defense, as is ordinarily required by law, after privately meeting with the judge. This law was never intended to be used in this fashion and violates fundamental rights of the defense to their own documents.

C. PROSECUTORIAL MISCONDUCT

During the selection of the jury the prosecutors engaged in ethnic cleansing, removing a number of younger and articulate African American jurors, while allowing older more docile African American jurors to sit. They then engaged in misconduct by, in effect, reminding the Miami jurors at the beginning of the trial that it was «us against them», and followed that with numerous unethical and improper comments, ending with a diatribe, repeated three times, that the Five had come from Cuba in order to «destroy the United States.»

All these issues are actively being litigated on appeal.

Conclusion

The case of the Five is one of the few cases in American jurisprudence that involves injustice at home as well as injustice abroad. Like the trial of the Pentagon Papers concerning the war in Vietnam, it derives from a failed foreign policy, which it exposes. In order to achieve a political end, the criminal justice system was then manipulated by the prosecutors who relentlessly violated legal norms.

The Five were not prosecuted because they violated American law, but because their work exposed those who were. By infiltrating the terror network that is allowed to exist in Florida they demonstrated the hypocrisy of America's claimed opposition to terrorism.

CHAPTER NINE

WAYNE S. SMITH

Wayne Smith is one of the country's most veteran Cuba watchers. He began working on Cuba in 1957 in the Department of State and was then transferred to Havana in July of 1958 as Third Secretary in the old American Embassy there. He remained until the rupture of relations in 1961, and then returned with the first group of American diplomats back into the country in April of 1977. He was Director of Cuban Affairs from 1977 until 1979, and then became Chief of the U.S. Interests Section from 1979 until 1982, when he left the Foreign Service because of his profound disagreements with the Reagan Administration's policies toward Cuba and in Central America. He is now an Adjunct Professor at the Johns Hopkins University in Baltimore and a Senior Fellow at the Center for International Policy in Washington, D.C.

A Sad Day in the History of American Justice: The Trial of the Cuban Five

I am not a lawyer, but I have had some experience with trials in Miami, having gone through one myself. Back in 1993, I was accused of libel by the Cuban American National Foundation (CANF). It was an absurd charge. As a friend who lived in Miami put it: "Only in Miami would the case even be considered. But if CANF wants to sue you, no one here is going to say 'no.'"

We asked for a change of venue, but it was denied. Of course. And so I was stuck with a jury trial in Miami (held in 1996), accused of saying something derogatory about the CANF. Not an enviable position to be in, given the charged atmosphere in Miami with respect to anything having to do with Cuba. But I remember saying to Alfredo Duran, an old friend and lawyer who had come forward to defend me: "Don't' worry Alfredo. I know you'll do a brilliant job. But no matter how good our case and how well you argue it, we're still almost certain to lose this round. But we'll win on appeal when it is a matter of law rather than political emotions."

And so it was. We lost the jury trial, but won an unqualified victory on appeal. Not surprisingly then, given that experience, my first comment on the trial of the Cuban Five, is that they never should have been tried in Miami. The atmosphere there was, and in many ways still is, quite different from the rest of the country. Polls taken in the year 2000, just before the trial began, for example, indicated that 49.7% of Cuban-Americans in Miami-Dade wanted to see direct U.S. military action against Cuba, as opposed to only 8.1 % of Americans throughout the country. [1] Many in the Cuban-American community at that time considered a state of war to exist with the Castro government. The Cuban Five, then, were seen as "enemies" and "agents of a hated foe" who of course had to be punished.

Attitudes have moderated over the past four years, but even now, Congressman Lincoln Diaz-Balart sets a certain tone with his public assertions that the U.S. should consider assassinating Fidel Castro. [2]

Miami, in short, is the last place in the United States that the Five should have been tried—whatever the charges against them. Their lawyers of course requested a change of venue, but it was denied. And precisely because the case was heard in Miami, the charges against them were blown out of all proportion. They were the unregistered agents of a foreign power, yes. That was a legitimate charge. Indeed, they confessed to it. Under normal circumstances, they would have been tried on that charge—and three of them perhaps for having false documents. The trial would have been over in a few days time and they would have been sentenced to relatively shorts jail terms.

Rather than that, they were also charged, in effect, with conspiracy to commit espionage. According to the prosecution, it was their intention to "communicate, deliver and transmit information relating to the national defense of the United States." [3]

The prosecution could present no evidence that they had in fact done any of those things. True, they were there in part to keep an eye on certain U.S. military bases from which attacks on Cuba might have been launched. But this was simply a matter of watching for and reporting any extraordinary build up that might have preceded an attack. It was not a matter of penetrating bases, stealing or otherwise obtaining secret information. It was, rather, a matter of observing what anyone else could have, and as the defense pointed out, this did not in any way rise to the level of "espionage." [4] Further, no such build-up ever took place, so they had nothing to observe. Neither did they seek or obtain a single classified document. They did not, in short, commit espionage, nor did the prosecution have a shred of evidence that they had. Its claim was that it was their intention at some point in the future to do so. Again, however, it had no real evidence of that. The claim was based largely on supposition and shouldn't have been considered.

The Five were also there—in fact, their principal mission was—to penetrate exile organizations and warn of terrorist efforts on their part against Cuba. As these were not official organizations, penetrating them was not a matter of espionage. Over many years, various exile organizations had advocated and carried out violent activities against Cuba. In 1997, bombs were detonated in several tourist hotels in Havana resulting in loss of life. These bombings were traced, in part by the Five, to Miami-based exiles. The Cuban government's information on the matter was shared with the FBI in hopes that the U.S. Government would take action against those responsible. Rather than that, this information sharing led to the arrest of the Five. No action was ever taken against the involved exiles. [5]

The most absurd, unjust and harmful charge of all was that against Gerardo Hernandez for first-degree murder conspiracy. This had to do with the shoot-down on February 24, 1996 of two Brothers-to-the-Rescue aircraft over the Straits of Florida. Supposedly, Hernandez was part of a conspiracy to bring down these planes, with the object of killing those aboard, with malice aforethought, in international airspace. [6]

This implies that there was some sort of secret plan to shoot the planes down. But nothing could be further from the truth. The Cuban government had warned that they would be shot down if they again penetrated Cuban airspace. Since 1995, BTTR aircraft had periodically violated Cuba airspace, even over-flying Cubans cities and in some cases dropping leaflets. I happened to be in Havana with a group of congressional staffers in January of 1996 when on the 9th and 13th, BTTR planes buzzed the city at very low altitudes dropping leaflets. We saw them on the 13th. An evening or two later, we were received by President Castro and brought up with him the over-flights and Cuba's reaction to them.

Castro made it clear that Cuba's patience had run out. BTTR had flagrantly and tauntingly violated Cuban airspace on numerous occasions, he said. Cuba had repeatedly warned the U.S. Government, but the latter had done nothing to stop the flights. Those on the 9th and 13th were the last straw ("el colmo"). The next time they violated Cuban airspace, they would risk being shot down.

One of the staffers commented that that might change the mood in the Congress and result in passage of the Helms-Burton bill (which then appeared to be stalled).

Castro said he hoped not. In fact, he hoped the U.S. would

take the necessary measures and that there would be no more flights. But the first duty of a government was to defend the national territory. Hence, he reasserted, if BTTR planes came in again, Cuba would take whatever action was deemed appropriate.

And indeed, the Cuban government presented a diplomatic note to the U.S. protesting the over-flights and noting that Cuba reserved the right to use force against any future violations of Cuban territory. This warning was repeated in open radio broadcasts.

Despite these warnings, Jose Basulto, the leader of BTTR, and the other BTTR pilots filed phony flights on February 24 and took off, headed for Cuba. About 3 p.m., approaching the 24th parallel, they were warned by Cuban Air Traffic Control that they were entering a restricted area which had been "activated." They were putting themselves in danger and should turn back. The warning was verbally acknowledged but ignored. [7]

They were then intercepted by Cuban Migs. Basulto's lead plane was well into Cuban airspace at that point. Both sides agree on that. According to Cuban radar fixes, the other two planes, the two that were shot down, were also in Cuban airspace. That is contradicted, however, by American radar fixes. According to those, the two planes had come within a couple of miles of Cuban territory, but were some 5 miles out when they were shot down.

Now, let me emphasize that I believe it was wrong to shoot the planes down, with the resulting loss of human lives—even had they been clearly within Cuban airspace. The Cubans would have done far better, even in terms of their own interests, to have warned them off by firing machine-gun bursts in front of the aircraft. They could then have taken the whole matter to the U.N. Security Council, pointing out that these illegal flights were creating a dangerous situation in the Straits of Florida, and calling on the Security Council to take cognizance. Cuba would then have had world public opinion on its side, and there would have been no tragic loss of life. Further, U.N. action might have stopped the over-flights.

But rather than that, the planes were shot down. Most regrettable. Still, it must be emphasized that they had been warned and that none of the Five encouraged them to fly. Certainly Gerardo Hernandez did not. True, there had been coded messages from Havana to members of the Five to discourage members of the Five who had infiltrated BTTR from flying, given the possibility of a confrontation. But everyone knew that possibility existed. Basulto and the others certainly knew it.. They were warned again in flight. They flew anyway.

Nor was Gerardo Hernandez—or anyone else of the Five—in anyway responsible for the shootdown. Indeed, as the defense pointed out: "The evidence concerning Hernandez's knowledge of and agreement to participate in an illegal plan to murder persons on board BTTR flights is wholly wanting." [8]

Despite this, he was found guilty and sentenced to life in prison—a gross miscarriage of justice. This seemed to result more than anything else from a quest for vengeance. Tempers were running high in Miami because of the shootdown and the deaths of the BTTR pilots. Someone had to pay. The axe fell on Hernandez, even though in fact he had nothing to do with it.

The vengeful anger was notable also in the treatment the Five after their arrest. For no discernible reason, they were held in tight solitary confinement for long periods of time, in widely separated prisons, in some cases not even permitted visits by their families.

The sentences were incredibly heavy—from 15 years to life imprisonment. As of this writing, they all remain in prison. It is to be hoped, however, that the appeals process—where it is a matter of law and not political emotions—will function as it should, resulting in a new trial, this time on proper charges—and now not in Miami.

CHAPTER TEN

SAUL LANDAU

Saul Landau is a former researcher of the U.S. State Department. He now directs the Digital Media Program at the California State Polytechnic University, Pomona.

His two new books are *The Pre-Emptive Empire: A Guide to Bush's Kingdom* and *The Business of America: How Consumers Have Replaced Citizens and We Can Reverse the Trend.*

Landau has produced more than fifty films on controversial themes ranging from portraits of Fidel Castro, Salvador Allende and Michael Manley to the Zapatista uprising in Chiapas, the US Congress, Sioux Indian rebellion at Wounded Knee and American jails. His latest film is Syria: Between Iraq and a Hard Place (2004).

He has written fourteen books, including *Assassination on Embassy Row*, on the murder of Orlando Letelier in 1976.

Five Cubans in Prison—Victims of Bush's Obsession

Think of the Cuban Five as victims of George W. Bush's obsessive-compulsive disorder. Facts: Five Cubans came to the United States undercover in the 1990s to infiltrate anti-Castro terrorist groups. They now occupy US prison cells. Cuban officials admit sending the agents because the FBI had failed to control violent activities aimed at Cuba. Instead of using information of terrorist plots provided by these agents, Justice Department prosecutors tried and convicted them on June 8, 2001 of espionage and complicity to murder.

Three years ago, at a Latin American Studies meeting, an anti-Castro Cuban scholar confided that, "the trial of Cuban spies in Florida could mean murder charges against the dictator." He gloated at the fantasy of bringing Fidel Castro before a US court.

"Grass will grow on my palm before that happens," I thought to myself. But Justice Department officials did actually begin to strategize about using the Cuban Five case to move against Castro. Guy Lewis, South Florida's US Attorney, even hinted that he might name Fidel as the master collaborator who supervised Gerardo Hernández, the alleged "spymaster." Hernández was convicted of accessory to murder four members of Brothers to the Rescue, an extreme anti-Castro group. Cuban MIGs shot down their two civilian planes on February 24, 1996 because, according to Lewis, the government proved "beyond any doubt there was a conspiracy to commit murder that had been approved of and ordered by the highest levels of the Cuban government."

In the Miami area, the US Attorney tends to follow the bidding of a variety of ultra right wing Cuban groups that comprise the anti-Castro lobby. Cuban American National Foundation (CANF) President Francisco Hernández elaborated on the US Attorney's remark. The "responsibility for the premeditated murder of four young men in the Brothers to the Rescue shoot down does not stop with the conviction of Gerardo Hernández. The next step," said Hernández, "is to indict those further up the chain of command who initiated this crime, including Fidel and Raul Castro. We call upon the Attorney General to take the necessary steps to bring all the guilty parties to justice."

The anti-Castro lobby's pressure to use the Cuban Five to get Castro worked. President Bush owes this small group of fanatic Castro haters not only for contributing heavily to his 2000 campaign, but for turning out voters early and often, whether or not they were US citizens, and then helping intimidate the Florida vote counters. They also helped re-elect his brother, Jeb, as Florida

Governor in 2002.

Bush began re-paying his debt even before 9/11. In his heart, Bush knew good terrorists from bad ones. And, in his decisive style, he issued orders, much like a spoiled child who knows what he wants and doesn't give a hoot about consequences: so, he wanted regime changes all over the world. His "get Castro" orders flowed from his inconsequential mouth as easily as his commands to make war with Afghanistan and Iraq. He lumped these policies together in the "fighting terrorism" and "advancing freedom" categories.

Granted that his decisiveness does not coincide with a large vocabulary, one should note the fervor and frequency of Bush's use of the words "terrorism" and "freedom." In Bush's April 13, 2004 press conference on Iraq he used "free" and "freedom" 50 times; "terror," "terrorists" and "terrorism" 30 times.

But recurrently as he has used the "f" and "t" words, Bush has never defined them. As a biblical aficionado—he likes to listen to other people read the Bible to him—Bush may well conceive of freedom to mean humanity's salvation (Armageddon and The Rapture that will follow) lies in the Middle East, an area he roughly understands as Afghanistan, Iraq, Syria and Palestine—Saudi Arabia of course enjoys special status thanks to the Bush family's business ties. Muslim terrorists (an extreme form of pagan) have become the enemy of freedom, while anti-Castro terrorists are freedom fighters.

So, when Bush exhorts the nation to fight terrorists, he means bad terrorists, not good ones. For example, the Bush White House spends eight times more to track Americans traveling to Cuba and to enforce a travel ban on that nation than for tracing Al-Qaeda financing. The FBI, which has allowed the fiendish anthrax case of 2001 to virtually drop into its cold case file, spent untold hours tracing the Cuban Five, who were themselves tracking terrorists.

The leaders of the anti-Castro cabal in South Florida, the

beneficiaries of Bush's "get Castro" policy, have also used the Cuba obsession to compulsively accumulate fortunes and political power. Before he died in 1997, Jorge Mas Canosa, founder and leader of CANF, had become one of the richest and most powerful figures in Florida. He attended regularly White House functions, had the ear of high officials and carte blanche to scores of congressional offices.

Bush's largesse extended to lesser fish as well. On May 20, 2002, the Secret Service allowed Sixto Reynaldo Aquit Manrique (a.k.a. El Chino Aquit) to sit a few rows behind the President on the platform as he spoke in Miami. The President's security detail knew that, on November 2, 1994, the FBI anti-terrorism squad nailed Aquit after he and two colleagues had "pulled up to a Southwest Dade warehouse…armed with 10 gallons of gas, fuses, and a loaded semiautomatic handgun." The November 4, 1994 *Miami Herald* story cited police saying, "the men smashed a window and tried to get inside before officers moved in."

A Florida court sentenced Aquit to five years in prison. Then, without explanation, the government accepted Aquit's guilty plea on a misdemeanor charge, which allowed him to skip prison and spend less than two years under house supervision. The government went soft on a man with a clear record of terrorism. You don't need Sherlock Holmes to find the reason. Aquit's terrorism was "patriotic zeal." He was a "good terrorist" who belonged to The Secret Armed Army, an anti-Castro group that advocates violence as the way to effect regime change in Cuba.

A year before his 1994 felony in Miami, Aquit fired a 50 caliber machine gun at a Cypriot tanker in Cuban waters. So, a good terrorist can sit close to the president without contradicting Bush's new security rules. Recall his September 20, 2001 address to Congress: "Either you are with us or you are with the terrorists." Trying to sink a cargo ship and burn down a warehouse does not constitute terrorism if done with anti-Castro intentions. Imagine an Abu Reinaldo Bin Aquit trying to sit near the President! The Secret Service would have shot him. But Bush directs his anti-terrorism compulsion at people with Islamic roots, not zealous, patriotic anti-Castro Cubans whose passion compels them to use violence—even in the United States.

Bush (43) also disregarded strong opinions from the FBI and INS when he ordered the freeing from INS deportation custody of Virgilio Paz and Jose Dionisio Suarez, both confessed conspirators in the 1976 car-bombing murders of former Chilean Chancellor Orlando Letelier and his US companion Ronni Moffitt in Washington DC.

President Bush and his brother Jeb continue to accept money and other campaign support from anti-Castro terrorists who have assassinated and bombed at will and yet seem virtually immune to prosecution in the United States. Since the 1970s, the FBI has possessed information linking CANF leaders to assassination, sabotage and other forms of terrorism directed at Cuba, but whose actual targets were located in Jamaica, Barbados, Mexico, Panama and the United States itself. CANF Chairman Mas Canosa and his organization grew richer and more politically connected.

On November 17, 2000, Panamanian authorities arrested four Cubans with records of extreme violence and close ties to CANF. Ranging in age from their mid fifties to early 70s, Luis Posada Carriles, Ignacio Novo Sampol, Pedro Remon and Gaspar Jimenez could have belonged to the old geezer wing assassins of the Foundation. Panamanian police found explosives in their rental car—with their fingerprints on the dangerous material. Cuban officials had tipped the Panamanians that these founding members of the "Kill Fidel" club had come to Panama to assassinate the Cuban President, who was attending a regional summit meeting there at the time.

Posada, the ringleader, had fled Cuba in 1959. He had served dictator Fulgencio Batista as a police agent. Most of his subsequent life he dedicated to attempting to assassinate Castro—working for the CIA and, in his own words, Jorge Mas Canosa.

In October 1976, Posada had colluded with fellow terrorist Orlando Bosch in bombing a Cuban passenger plan over Barbados. Like Posada, Bosch had boasted of his role in that act of terrorism, in which 73 people died.

Venezuelan authorities arrested both men, but Posada prevailed on his pal Mas to shell out $50 thousand to bribe prison authorities. After he busted Posada out of the Venezuelan prison, Mas got his terrorist buddy a job with Lt. Col. Oliver North, who hired the fugitive to work on the Contra campaign in Central America, an activity over which Vice President Bush exercised more than casual control. Unknown gunmen shot Posada in the face in Guatemala in February 1990. When he recovered, he began his terrorism against tourism campaign in Cuba. Indeed, he boasted to a *New York Times* (July 12) reporter in 1998 that Mas had helped finance his campaign to bomb tourist spots in Cuba in the mid 1990s to discourage tourism. One bombing led to the death of an Italian tourist.

That same *New York Times* reports that "with a rueful chuckle, Posada described the Italian tourist's death as a freak accident, but he declared that he had a clear conscience, saying, 'I sleep like a baby.' 'It is sad that someone is dead, but we can't stop,' he added. 'That Italian was sitting in the wrong place at the wrong time.'"

On April 20, 2004, a Panamanian court found Posada and the other defendants guilty of threatening public security and falsifying documents—not attempted assassination of Castro. Posada got 8-years in prison. Novo and Remon received 7-year sentences and Jimenez received 8.

Even though Havana criticized the leniency of the sentences, these convictions mark a rare turn of events. Anti-Castro terrorists had received a near carte blanche from the White House, thanks to the political power of the Cuba lobby.

Indeed, the US government's coddling of terrorists bent on doing damage to Cuba motivated Cuban intelligence to send infiltrators to Miami. At their trial, the court-appointed attorneys for the Cuban agents argued that in light of decades of terrorist actions carried out against Cuba from US soil and the FBI's less than enthusiastic persecution of the anti-Castro terrorists, Havana had sent in the spies to infiltrate extremist exile groups out of self defense, to stop future violent actions in Cuba.

The defense chose a 12-member non-Cuban jury with no close Cuban relatives or friends to remove social pressure from the verdict in the largest Cuban community off the communist island. But the intimidation factor worked nonetheless. One would have to be either ignorant or deaf, dumb and blind not to know about the reputation in that area of violent Cuban exiles; not exactly the kind of people who make for a fair trial climate. South Florida juries have become notorious for their consistency in deciding against the Castro government.

After six months of trial, the jury deliberated for four days before declaring the five Cuban agents guilty of violating US espionage laws and Hernández of collaborating in the shoot down of the Brothers to the Rescue planes.

Cuba argued that the MIGs fired over Cuban airspace after Cuba's air control had ordered the pilots not to enter its air space. Washington countered that the planes were in international air space when the missiles hit their targets. At the trial, the spies' lawyers presented testimony to show that the Cuban government had warned US authorities over a period of almost two years during which the Brothers had continually over-flown Cuba, including missions when they dropped leaflets.

The Cuban spies acknowledged they had infiltrated the Brothers and that the Havana spymaster had warned the infiltrator not to fly in the period when the fatal shoot down occurred. The prosecution argued that such advice meant aiding and abetting a cold-blooded murder. But, the jury also learned, high US officials had foreknowledge of the impending flights and even warned Havana about them.

The defense offered abundant evidence to show the logic of Cuba's fear of the extremist groups in South Florida. Few feigned surprise, however, when the jury found all five defendants guilty of operating as foreign agents without notifying the US government and conspiring to do so. Three were convicted of conspiracy to commit espionage and for efforts to penetrate US military bases. Hernández received a life sentence on the conspiracy count.

Among a small sector of Miami, anti-Castro fixation overwhelms other events and stands out as a glaring exception to Bush's war on terrorism. "Nuclear war could break out and CANF would plot to make it seem as if Fidel was responsible," quipped a Cuban diplomat. Fidel exported these crackpots to the United States and Bush has agreed to share their Castro obsession. Democratic Presidential candidate John Kerry, who declared his intention to get tough on Castro if he wins, shows that he, too, will bow to the idiocy of the small group of ultra right wing Cuban exiles who have clutched US-Cuba policy in their intimidating fists.

Meanwhile, five brave Cubans sit in US prisons. Will it require that medical science perfect the spinal transplant to get a president to take back Cuba policy from the rabid exiles?

CHAPTER ELEVEN

MICHAEL STEVEN SMITH

Michael Steven Smith is an attorney and author in New York City. He has testified on human rights issues before committees of the United States Congress and the United Nations. He is the co-editor with Michael Ratner of *Che Guevara and the FBI*, co-editor of *The Emerging Police State* by William Kunstler, editor of *Defending Cuba and the Cuban Five*, and author of a memoir *Notebook of a Sixties Lawyer*.

A Tale of Two Law Suits

This is the tale of two lawsuits, the first, the case of the Cuban Five, a criminal case prosecuted by the United States government in Miami in 1998 and the second, The People of Cuba versus The Government of the United States, brought a year later in Havana. For the Cubans in both cases it was the worst of times, because they lost, but in a sense, it was the best of times in that the moral authority of the Cuban revolution in contrast to the hypocrisy of the American government's "war on terrorism" has been shown for all to see.

Political times have emblematic cases. The ongoing Mumia case, Lynne Stewart's current prosecution, and the two cases involving the U.S. and Cuban governments illuminate the reality of today's politics in America just as the Sacco Vanzetti case in the 1920s with respect to immigrants and anarchists or the McCarthyite anti-communist Rosenberg case in the 1950s defined their eras.

The appeals of the Cuban Five's convictions were orally argued by Leonard Weinglass and other attorneys in April of 2004 in Miami. Two of the Five are doing life sentences, one is doing two life sentences, another was sentenced to nineteen years, and the last got off easy with seventeen behind bars. They are separated in five of the worst prisons in America.

The Cuban Five were convicted of conspiracy to commit espionage. The U.S. government frequently charges "conspiracy", it is like a thought crime. One was convicted of conspiracy to commit murder. All were convicted of minor charges including failing to register as agents of a foreign government. The convictions came about in this way. When the Soviet Union went under in 1991 Cuba was in a lot of trouble economically. It had lost its lifeline. The Cubans thought that if they developed their tourist industry they could get some hard currency coming into the country. Cuba is a beautiful island. It is as large as the rest of the Caribbean combined. It has gorgeous beaches, Havana is lovely, especially Old Havana, with its 18th century buildings constructed at a time when Havana was the great city in the western hemisphere. So Cuba got people from places like Spain, Germany, and Italy to travel there on vacation. The plan was really working.

This all didn't sit well with the terrorists the United States coddles in Miami. This "Mafia," as they are referred to by the Cubans, thought that if they could stop the tourism in Cuba, they could really weaken the government there paving the way for its overthrow. If Emma Lazarus was to write a poem for a new statue of liberty for the Port Everglades, which is the harbor serving South Florida, the poem might read as follows: "Give me your terrorists/ your country sellers/ your capitalist restorationists/ your assassins/ your torturers/ your scum of the earth." Of the six hundred and fifty thousand persons of Cuban descent who live in Miami there are more than a few who would fit that description. Orlando Bosch lives there. He walks his dog every morning. This man killed seventy-three persons, including the young Cuban fencing team, when he blew up a Cuban airliner. Felix Rodriguez and Alberto Gonzales, live there as well in comfortable retirement. They were the two CIA contract agents who directed the capture and murder of Che Guevara in Bolivia. Rodriguez, a friend of George Bush the first, went on to participate in the contra-wars in Central America in the 1980s. A number of terrorists in South Florida openly train in the Everglades.

What they did was to start attacking the Cuban tourist economy. The planted a bomb in a hotel which killed an Italian tourist. They planted bombs on a bus coming from the Havana airport and tried to bomb the airport itself. The Cuban government, to try to stop this, pleaded with the U.S. government to put a stop to it. When the U.S. didn't the Cubans sent five young men—the cream of the Cuban revolution—secretly to Miami under assumed names to infiltrate the terrorist organizations, which they did. They compiled large dossiers on the terrorist groups. The number two man in the FBI met with his Cuban counterpart in the Interior Ministry and the Cubans turned the dossiers over to the United States and reiterated its demand that they put a stop to the terror; after all there is an American law called the Neutrality Act which prohibits attacks on foreign countries with whom we are at peace launched from American soil. So the Cubans requested that the Americans call a halt, that they please stop the Miami mafia.

What did the American government do? It arrested the five Cubans and tried them in Miami, of all places. This prejudicial venue calls to mind a story circulating in Havana when the Pope visited Castro some years ago. He was riding with Fidel in the open popemobile along the Malecon, along the ocean, when a breeze stirred up and lifted the Pope's little skullcap of his head. It floated in the air and landed in the ocean about fifty feet from the shore. Fidel asked the driver to stop the limo. He said to the Pope, "Papa, I will get your cap back." Fidel then got out of the popemobile, walked over to the shoreline, and then he walked across the top of the water fifty feet, picked up the skull cap, and then walked back across the water to the limo and placed the skull cap back atop

Papa's head. This event was reported as follows: Prensa Latina, the Cuban newspaper, ran an article recounting the events pretty much as just stated. La Observatoire Romano, the newspaper of the Vatican, reported in its headline that "Pope Allows Castro to Perform Miracle." And finally, the Miami Herald, in screaming second coming type forty point typed ran a headline proclaiming "Castro: Too Old to Swim." You can't get a break in Miami.

The Judge for The Miami Five trial has a husband who is the city attorney for North Miami. If she would have allowed a changed of venue, which is granted routinely, after all, the man who bombed the Federal building in Oklahoma City was tried in Denver, racist cops in Brooklyn are tried in Albany, her husband wouldn't have gotten re-elected. The defense lawyers requested that the trial be moved, not out of state, but just thirty miles up the coast to Fort Lauderdale. The judge said no. It is impossible to get a fair trial in Miami if you are Cuban revolutionary. Remember the atmosphere surrounding six-year-old Elian Gonzalez whom the gusanos refused to return to his communist father.

The trial took seven months. The jury was out but three and a half days before they found the Five guilty of everything. The jury was contaminated necessarily because it was a Miami jury. The foreman during the voir dire said he believed Castro to be a communist dictator and that he would be happy the day he was thrown out. The daughter of another juror worked for the FBI for ten years, his son was a Marine for twenty-one years, and he opined that the whole Cuban government was incompatible with his experiences as a retired banker. A third juror was married to a member of the Pedro Pan brigade, young children sent from Cuba to Miami, with the support of the Catholic church, to flee escaped atheistic communism. Another juror was married to an immigration guard and so on. The whole jury was like that. The Five received horrific sentences. This is what is on appeal.

The facts and law in the case, in Weinglass' opinion, are very strong in favor of the Five. There was insufficient evidence to send someone to prison for conspiracy to commit espionage when they didn't take one single page of anything that was classified. It was all public information. Gerardo Hernandez, who was convicted for conspiracy to commit murder, had infiltrated The Brothers to the Rescue outfit that had flown multiple flights low over Havana dropping leaflets. They had discussed flying a drone equipped with explosives to kill Fidel when he spoke at an outdoor rally. Two planes, after repeated Cuban warnings to the U.S., were shot down. Hernandez didn't event know this. He was merely told not to fly that day. The government of Cuba shot down the planes as an act of state. This is the first time in history that someone has been convicted because of an act of state.

The necessity defense, which allows for a small crime if it is done to stop a larger one, was not allowed by the Judge to be raised. The sentences were absolutely savage. Aldrich Ames and Robert Hanson, who are also doing life sentences, stole thousands of documents and compromised American security. The Cuban Five didn't steal one. Yet they got the same sentences. And their crime remember was conspiracy to commit espionage some time in the future.

What will happen? What will the Court of Appeals for the Eleventh Circuit—not the most distinguished court—rule in the fall of this year? It is very hard to get justice in the present climate. It is a cold comfort to know that Governor Dukakis of Massachusetts exonerated Sacco and Vanzetti. The Rosenbergs were innocent of conspiracy to steal the secret of he atomic bomb, as we now know. There was no secret. Making an "A" bomb was a question of industrial capacity. The Cuban Five have been branded as terrorists as well as communists. In the fearful atmosphere that has pervaded since 9/11 we cannot be sure the judges will do the right thing. The case has not received the attention it should have. So what we can do is publicize their situation and offer our solidarity.

* * *

A year after the U.S. government succeeded in salting away the Cuban Five the U.S. government itself was sued by the people of Cuba. The lawsuit was brought on behalf of eight organizations in Cuba, the trade unions, the small farmers, the women's organization, the children, the Committees to Defend the Revolution, and the veterans. These organizations make up most of the Cuban population.

The suit alleged and identified acts of aggression by the U.S., its agents, servants, and employees from the period of 1960 to 1999—that is for forty years. It does not mention what the U.S. did from 1956, when the motor yacht Granma landed with Fidel and the others who began the movement that eventually overthrew Batista. It doesn't mention the fact that the U.S. trained, armed, and supplied the soldiers of the Batista dictatorship. It doesn't mention the 20,000 Cubans who lost their lives in the Cuban war for independence. It doesn't start there.

It starts instead in 1960 with a list of what has been done the Cuban people. One cold statistic stands out: in the period of 1960 to 1999, the suit states, the U.S. government has been responsible for killing 3478 persons in Cuba and it has been responsible for bodily injuring 2099 people. It is those incidents of injuring and killing that the lawsuit covers.

The suit addresses the practice of biological warfare. The U.S. government says it is against biological warfare and it would never use it. Yet Fort Detrick in Maryland is the biggest biological warfare armory in the world. The suit alleged that it was in Fort Detrick that the mosquito was developed that carries Dengue 2 fever.

Dengue 2 causes internal hemorrhaging. The suit stated that it was an agent of the U.S. that brought the Dengue 2-carrying insect into Cuba, which caused 24,000 people to hemorrhage.

When a person bleeds internally they lose blood. People need blood to bring oxygen to nourish the brain. It they don't have enough blood going to the brain they go into shock—and in Cuba 10,224 people went into shock.

Prolonged shock causes death. Who dies easiest? Children. One hundred and fifty-eight people died, and of those 101 were children, killed by the U.S. with Dengue 2 fever. The U.S. didn't confine itself to killing people. It thought it could attack Cuba's food supply and brought in African Swine Fever—a disease, like Dengue 2, that had never been present in Cuba before. The Cubans had to do away with 500,000 pigs to prevent further spread of the disease. Tobacco blight was another disease that the U.S. brought in.

When the revolution succeeded on January 1, 1959, one of the first things that the revolutionary government did was to create a law—which was very popular because a lot of people who had fought on the side of the revolution benefited directly from it—initiating a comprehensive land reform. Previously, large tracts of land had been owned by American corporations. The average Cuban peasant worked part time, seasonally, was not literate, and lived from hand to mouth. What the revolutionary government did was to nationalize these big properties—which was their right under international law. Not only did they nationalize them. They told the former owners that they would be compensated for their losses. The said to the American owners: "We will pay you exactly the amount you said they were worth when you listed them for tax purposes." But they were turned down.

In retaliation, the United States, which was refining all of Cuba's oil in American-owned oil refineries, stopped refining oil, and Cuba was cut off from gasoline. What did the Cubans do? They nationalized the refineries, and willy-nilly, the bus company was nationalized, the phone company was nationalized, the nickel mines were nationalized, the economy was rationalized. Instead of having production for profit, which is really irrational, anarchical, they had a planned economy—that's what is called a socialist revolution. That's what happened very quickly, to America's surprise, in Cuba. And getting that property back has been the aim of American foreign policy ever since.

What was the response of the U.S? They initiated the blockade. It was not started before the missile crisis in 1962. It was back in 1960, just after the revolution, and it has been consistently and every more stringently been applied since.

One of the first things the revolutionary government did was to send people out into the countryside on a literacy campaign so that all the Cubans could learn how to read and write. Literacy is after all a necessity for a better life and the sine qua non of democracy and self-rule. The U.S. government, the law suit alleged, supported terrorists who murdered the teachers.

The U.S. government, the Cuban's charged, had a similar policy against the collective farms. When the collective farms were organized the suit contended that the U.S. supported groups who set fire to the sugar crops, killing people in the process. That was documented in the lawsuit.

In the U.S. we have what is called common law—under which a lawsuit is begun by first making allegations and then the initiator of the lawsuit has the burden of proving the allegations at trial. In Cuba it is different. The plaintiffs must submit proof with their allegations. So appended to the complaint of the Cubans is proof of what they are claiming, much of it in documents the U.S. government itself released.

American policy killed or injured over 5000 people and that is not to speak of the hundreds of thousands of persons who had and have to live with the psychological burden of having this beast 90 miles north of them waging continual aggression. So there was a psychological aspect to the suit too. In the U.S. it is called "the intentional infliction of emotional distress," and there was a demand for compensation for this also.

The Cubans brought the lawsuit in Havana and although the U.S. was duly served through its Interest Section the U.S. refused to appear as a defendant. The Cubans then presented their evidence at a trial. Attorney and journalist William Schaap of New York attended the trial. He wrote that "It is difficult to convey the poignancy and power of the personal testimony of the hundreds of eyewitnesses who recounted these horrors. In describing the five year war against the (U.S. supported) bandits in the countryside, men and women, now in their 80s told of seeing their children tortured and killed before their eyes. Likewise, children, now in their 40s and 50s, described the deaths of their parents at the hands of the bandits. Aging veterans of the peasant militia—many of whom had never held a weapon until they took up arms against the bandits—showed the court, and the Cuban television audience, their horrible wounds, the maimed or missing limbs. Some spoke of suffering mental illness for decades, of nightmares and insomnias."

The trial ended with the Cubans being granted a judgment by default, a judgment yet to be collected. Why didn't the Cubans proceed against the U.S. by bringing suit in The World Court? Because the U.S. was hauled in front of The World Court for mining the harbor in Nicaragua and for supplying the Contras in the 1980s. A judgment was awarded to the Nicaraguans causing the U.S. to pull out of The World Court. They don't recognize The World Court anymore.

The U.S. has shown in both these suits to be a country dishonoring the rule of law, substituting instead its own notion of American might. This arrogance has most recently been asserted, earning the contempt of much of the world, in the U.S. illegal war against and occupation of Iraq. Meanwhile the fate of the Cuban Five will be decided by 11th Circuit Court of Appeals in Miami in the fall of 2004. Justice and fairness demand the reversal of these brave mens' convictions. The U.S. has yet again the chance to do the right thing with respect to Cuba and its people.

The Cuban website on the Cuban Five and terrorism is: www.antiterroristas.cu and the Free the Five Defense Committee's website is www.freethefive.org

CHAPTER TWELVE

JAMES PETRAS

James Petras was a member of the Bertrand Russell Tribunal against repression in Latin America (1973-76). He was a student leader in Berkeley in the 1960s.

From 1965 to 1973 he worked in Chile and was an adviser to the Allende government from 1970 to 1973. His book *The U.S. and the Overthrow of Allende* is considered required reading.

He has lectured at universities and worked with popular movements throughout Latin America, Europe, Asia and Oceania.

He is the author and editor of 63 books translated in 21 languages.

He is currently an adviser to the landless workers movement in Brazil and adjunct professor at Saint Mary's University in Canada and professor emeritus at SUNY Binghamton University.

The Cuban Five: Nominees for the Nobel Peace Prize

In the struggle against terrorism, the Cuban Five stand out as worthy candidates for a Nobel Peace Prize. The terrorists are largely Cuban exiles located in Miami and financed by the U.S. Government and backed by the Cuban-American Foundation, the Presidents of the United States and of course the U.S. intelligence agencies over the past 45 years. These terrorists have bombed airliners, assassinated Cuban farmers as well as diplomats, European tourists and Cuban-American critics in Florida and Puerto Rico among many and diverse victims. They of course function with total impunity in the United States.

The principal center for U.S. backed exile terrorism is the Cuban-American Foundation (CAF), which is the channel for funding terrorist actions directed against Cuba. All U.S. Democratic and Republican presidential candidates appeal to the CAF for electoral support, in exchange for promoting political and economic legislation designed to destroy the Cuban economy. Thanks to Cuba's world-class security system and intelligence forces, most of the terrorist plots have been foiled saving thousands of innocent lives.

The Clinton Presidency tolerated the CAF sponsored attacks on Cuba's tourist economy—the principal source of Cuba's foreign exchange. In response, the Revolutionary Government decided to form a counter-terrorism team in order to gather information within the United States on Cuban exile based terrorist plots and defend itself. The "Cuban Five" assumed the task of infiltrating the exile terrorists groups in order to inform Cuban authorities on impending violent activities, including plots to assassinate Cuban leaders and diplomats, the bombing of tourist hotels and restaurants. Collecting information on terrorist groups plotting to commit acts of violence is accepted national security policy the world over. The Cuban Five played an exemplary role in the world-wide struggle against terrorism—its intelligence allowed Cuban authorities to capture would-be terrorists, before or during planned assaults and to identify and neutralize maritime attacks and aerial violations of Cuban air space.

Cuban intelligence, thanks to information from the "Cuban Five" was able to facilitate the arrest of several leading exile terrorists who had planned to bomb a packed university auditorium in Panama where thousands of students were scheduled to hear a speech by Fidel Castro. The "Cuban Five" counter-terrorist activities not only saved Cuban lives but also provided a service to independent political leaders and activists throughout the world who opposed U.S. imperialist ambitions. Miami-based terrorists working with the CIA were involved in the murder of former Chilean Defense Minister Orlando Letelier and his American assistant in 1975 in Washington DC; they tortured and murdered the world-revered guerrilla leader Che Guevara in Bolivia and they were deeply involved with the Nicaraguan mercenaries (1980-1990), El Salvador and Honduras death squads and the Guatemalan genocide (1980-1984) of the Mayan Indians. By keeping track of these international terrorists and providing timely information to Cuban intelligence Havana was able to warn governments in Latin America of planned terrorist incidents.

The U.S. government arrested the Cuban Five not for 'spying' (they never spied on U.S. civilian or military installations) but for disrupting their Miami-based terror network. The Cuban Five exposed the hypocrisy of Washington's so-called "anti-terrorists policies" before, during and after September 11, 2001. The U.S. regime used the anti-terrorist information provided by Cuban intelligence (much of it provided by the 'Cuban 5' themselves) to identify and arrest the Cuban 5 thus giving the exile terrorists a free hand in continuing their attacks on civilian targets inside Cuba and in order to intimidate business investors and European and Canadian tourists visiting Cuba.

The U.S. attack on Cuba's anti-terrorist agents was a signal to terrorists the world over, that if they acted for U.S. imperial interests and against U.S. adversaries and critics they would be untouchable. Ariel Sharon understood that message when he pursued the "selective assassinations" of hundreds of Palestinian leaders and opponents—knowing in advance that Washington would approve. U.S. military 'interrogators'-torturers in Iraq received the message as they murdered jailed resistance activists throughout Iraq.

Washington's alliance with and financing and training of violent terrorist gangs has a long and ignoble history—and it has come at a terrible cost to U.S. citizens. At the end of World War Two, the U.S. government worked closely with the Sicilian mafia led by Lucky Luciano to decimate the left wing anti-fascist forces in Southern Italy, thus strengthening the criminal gangs (really private armies) which would dominate the major ports, road transport and construction unions and related industries in the U.S. in addition to promoting prostitution, drugs and political corruption. During the 1950's the United States allied itself with the terrorist dictatorships in Haiti, Dominican Republic, Cuba, Peru and Venezuela to secure compliant clients in the Cold War and control over strategic materials, resulting in the growth of anti-imperialist movements and the success of the Cuban revolution. In the 1960's the United States developed ties with the drug traffickers in Southeast Asia and death squads in Vietnam in an effort to defeat the Indo-Chinese revolution, resulting in military defeat and the exponential growth and export of drugs into the United States. In the 1970's the United States under President Carter recruited, trained, armed and financed a large number of Islamic fundamentalists from around the world to invade and attack the secular republic of Afghanistan, the same forces which later flew airliners into the Twin Towers in New York and the Pentagon in Washington. In the 1980's and 1990's Washington militarily supported Muslim extremists and mafia gangsters who fought in Bosnia, Chechnya and Kosova against the Serbs and Russians, reaping a new group of future fighters against Washington and its European partners.

In every instance, Washington's support for terrorists, whether Sicilian mobsters, Moslem fundamentalists, Latin dictators or Israeli state-assassins, has boomeranged; the terrorists turned against their paymasters or kindled the fire of radical anti-imperialist revolts. When and if the United States normalizes relations with Cuba, we will have on our hands—within this country—a well-trained, ruthless group of Cuban-American terrorists fully capable of turning their sights on U.S. targets.

The Cuban Five were engaged in non-violent preventive action—intelligence gathering directed toward avoiding new conflicts and tensions between the United States and Cuba. The Cuban Five were acting to further deepen and extend the burgeoning people-to-people, business-to-business relations, which were growing by leaps and bounds from the mid-1990's to the present (2004). Agricultural exporters in 34 states in the Union were selling over 500 million dollars in foods and animal grains to Cuba; hundreds of thousands of U.S. visitors, including Cuban-Americans were visiting each year, despite the travel restrictions. Increasingly Washington's economic and travel blockade was eroding; outside of Miami and Washington there was little support for the anti-Cuban policies and even less for the terrorist exile cells planting bombs in hotels, airliners and school auditoriums. Public opinion polls showed that over two-thirds of U.S. citizens were opposed to travel restrictions and the economic embargo. Even the Cuban American community was hostile to terrorists "all or nothing" approach to Cuban-U.S. relations. The Cuban Five's preventive anti-terrorist activity was vital to the growing 'rapprochement' between the United States and Cuba—as it contributed to stabilizing the political climate thus promoting market and cultural exchanges.

During the Bush Presidency, the United States has pursued an aggressive policy of recruiting and financing agents in Cuba as well as imposing more stringent restrictions on family remittances and cultural exchanges. Washington has sought to foment internal discord, as its terrorist allies in Miami plot unimpeded, now that Cuban anti-terrorists have been jailed. The fear of many experts on U.S.-Cuban relations is that the Bush Administration may use its Miami-based terrorist network to provoke an 'incident' or violent attack to escalate U.S. aggression in line with the Bush Doctrine of "permanent wars" against independent Third World countries.

In a deeper sense the Cuban Five risked their freedom for the principles of the United Nations Charter—"the right of countries to self-determination", the right of a people to decide its own form of government, and the universal right to defend itself against outside aggressors whose purpose is to impose its rule by force and terror. By acting against U.S. backed Cuban-American terrorist gangs, the Cuban Five were upholding their right of the Cuban people to decide for themselves their present and future form of governance. Among the vast majority of Cuban and Latin American peoples the Cuban Five are seen as heroes, who dared to enter the territory of the imperial heartland and expose the violent machinations of its terrorist protégés. By arresting and prosecuting these counter-terrorist Latin American patriots under the most prejudicial circumstances and sentencing these heroic men, all fathers and husbands, to virtual life sentences in solitary confinement, Washington has once more demonstrated that in the underworld of terror, it has no restraints, no shame, and no fear—except when its own creations turn against them and we, the citizens of the United States, suffer the ugly consequences.

CHAPTER THIRTEEN

JITENDRA SHARMA

Jitendra Sharma is the president of the International Association of Democratic Lawyers. This association has representatives at the UNESCO and the UNICEF and is recognized as a consultive entity in the United Nations.

It has members in 96 countries.

Real Fighters Against Terrorism

Terrorism has affected the lives of the people throughout the world. It has caused untold misery, death, disablement, kidnapping, rape and tremendous loss of property. People have lost not only their near and dear ones but have been deprived of their homes, hearth and shelters. The terrorism has rendered millions orphan, lonely and homeless.

Terrorist strike on 11th September 2001 at the twin towers of the World Trade Centre in New York and Pentagon at Washington etc. was terrible. Thousands of innocent people became victims of terrorism. The people around the world sympathized with the families who lost their loved ones. They condoled with them for their irreparable loss. Most people were shocked. They were dazed by the audacity of the terrorist strike. The mightiest of the mighty, the United States of America has been hit where it hurts most. Its pride was lost, damaged and destroyed. The symbol of economic power and prosperity of the United States, the Twin Towers, were no more. The source of power of US imperialism, the Pentagon in Arlington lay in shambles. The same Pentagon which evokes awe and fear in different parts of the world, a symbol of its military might, could not protect itself. The headquarters of the US Department of Defense could not be defended against a terrorist attack.

It was not the first time that terrorism raised its ugly head. The terrorists have caused havoc for decades in different parts of the world. It was sheer enormity of the crime that shook the world. Due to unfortunate and wholly unnecessary enormous loss of life and property, September 11 terrorist attack sharply focused the world attention to the dangers of terrorism.

India has been a victim of terrorism for a long time. Mrs. Indira Gandhi, the then Prime Minister of India was shot dead by the Punjab Terrorists. Her son, Mr. Rajiv Gandhi who became the Prime Minister of India after Indira Gandhi's assassination was later killed by Sri Lankan Tamil militants. India has lived for over two decades with Punjabi Terrorists, Kashmiri militants with different outfits and flags, and terrorism in its Northeastern part. Last addition to terrorism in India was a spill over of strife between Tamil Tigers and Sri Lankan Government. Several thousands of Indian have lost their lives due to terrorism. Property worth billions of Dollars has been destroyed.

What has come to be known as Kashmir terrorism is largely a result of cross-border terrorism. These terrorists are known to have been trained, armed and financed by Pakistan. They have their training camps and, bases across the border, mainly in what is known as "Pakistan occupied Kashmir". There are daily attacks on various targets by different terrorist outfits resulting in continuous loss of life. In December 2002 they attacked the India's Parliament House killing a number of police personnel. There is a long history of terrorist violence in India and unfortunately most of it is aided and abetted from outside the country.

Like India, Cuba has been a constant target of terrorism. Ever since the victory of the Cuban Revolution in January, 1959 terrorist activities are being systematically carried out against Cuba by counter revolutionaries who are aided and abetted by the United States.

Cuba during the last 45 years has faced economic blockade enforced by successive US administrations in an attempt to strangulate Cuba and its economy. During this period thousands of terrorist acts have been committed against Cuba. Over 600 attempts have been made to assassinate President Fidel Castro. Amongst the terrorist violence is the blowing up of a Cuban Airlines plane in-mid air killing all the 73 passengers and crew, attack on several hotels in Havana during the World Festival of Youth and Students and every conceivable form of attack on Cuban infrastructure. These terrorist attacks became particularly more intense after the collapse of the Soviet Union.

Most of these attacks have been launched from Miami, which is the center of all illegal activities carried out by Cuban American "exiles" against Cuba.

Gerardo Hernandez, Ramon Labanino, Fernando Gonzalez Antonio Guerrero and Rene Gonzalez, all Cubans, two of them holding US Citizenship, were arrested on 12th September 1998. For 17 months since after their arrest they were kept in solitary confinement. They were held incommunicado and were not allowed to have any contact or communication with their families, attorneys or amongst themselves.

Even though there were 26 specific offences alleged against them but most were minor relating to use of false identify etc. The most serious charge against them was alleging conspiracy to commit espionage while Gerardo Hernandez was later further accused of conspiracy to commit murder. Both these charges if proved invited life sentence.

What has been the basis of these changes?

Miami is the centre of terrorist activities against Cuba. It has a large number of Cuban "exiles" who consistently not only carry on anti-Cuba and anti-Castro campaign but resort to naked terrorism. They control public opinion on any issue involving Cuba and wield enormous political and economic power. Many of the leaders of the anti-Cuba lobby were in the 1960s and 70s were trained by CIA to carry out terrorist acts of sabotage shooting and bombing. Their activities have resulted in the killing of over 4000 Cubans.

Since most of the anti-Cuba terrorist activities were being planned and executed by the various terrorist organizations from Miami, it became essential for Cuba for its self—defense to have information in respect of such illegal terrorist activities. This was one way of protecting Cuba and its people from becoming victims of terrorist violence. These five young Cubans considered it their patriotic duty to get as much information about the nefarious activities of these anti-Cuban terrorists. They infiltrated the ranks of the anti Cuban groups in Miami, obtained information about their planned terrorist activities and relayed the same to Cuba so that preventive steps against such acts would be taken. This became all the more necessary as United States Administration has always been unwilling to extend any cooperation and was in fact fully supporting and conniving with the activities of these terrorist outfits in Miami. One of the world's most notorious terrorists, Luis Posada Carriles, together with Orlando Bosch, had their base in Miami where they planned and financed their dastardly actions against Cuba.

The strategy of seeking information from within the terrorist groups themselves is a well-recognized method in anti-terrorist operations adopted by all the countries. Even the US Intelligence Agencies have adopted this method after the terrorist strikes of September 11. Cuba shared with the US Administration the information that they gathered on the plans of these terrorist organizations. However, the US response to the sharing of information by Cuba, was of total unconcern and inaction. On the contrary it altered the anti-Cuba terrorist groups that their ranks have been infiltrated as information about their plans are being leaked out to Cuba. Moreover instead of extending any cooperation to Cuba, the US administration, after getting information about their commendable role arrested these five young Cuban patriots.

The charge of conspiracy to murder against Gerardo Hernandez was that the two planes belonging to the Miami based anti-Cuban organization, "Brothers to the Rescue" were shot down by the Cuban Armed Forces when they violated Cuban air space and refused to return despite warning. Four of the terrorists on board these planes perished. Hernandez was at that time in Miami. He was not involved in making or executing the order to shoot down the planes. It was clear that Gerardo Hernandez was not responsible for the death of the four men in the two planes. It was established during the trial that light aircrafts used by the terrorists had made repeated violations of Cuban air space to perpetuate numerous violent and terrorist acts including shooting, bombing and dropping of chemical and bacteriological substances. The shooting of the two planes was an independent lawful act of a sovereign state of Cuba to protect its air space and an act fully legal and valid both under the international law as well as the domestic law of Cuba. It was also established that Cuba had previously warned that it will not tolerate any further incursions into its air space.

They were put on trial in Miami a place where the possibility of getting justice for any one even remotely sympathetic to Cuba was non-existent. These terrorist gangs in Miami had perpetuated innumerable crimes and killings in the United States and mainly Miami against institutions or individuals who were connected to Cuba or stood for establishment of normal relations between United States and Cuba. In this atmosphere it was impossible for these five Cubans to get any justice in Miami. They made repeated motions to move the trial outside Miami. They did not even insist on shifting it outside the State of Florida. Their request to shift the trial even to a place, 50 kilometers away from Miami, where the population was heterogeneous was turned down.

The world has not forgotten the violence, threat and intimidation carried out by these terrorist gangs when Elian Gonzalez, a six-year-old Cuban boy was kidnapped and held hostage in Miami. These terrorist groups had indulged in violence, destroyed property, burnt US flag and threatened to burn the city if the child was sought to be returned to Cuba. The extent of their political clout can be seen from the fact that even the Mayor of Miami refused to implement the Federal order to restore Elian Gonzalez to his father. It was in this background and atmosphere that these five were put to trial in Miami.

During the trial, the five accused had clearly stated that they were working for the Cuban Government to protect Cuba from terrorist attacks which are organized and launched from Miami and for that purpose they had infiltrated some of the Miami based Cuban—American organizations, which were organizing these actions.

They made it clear that they had not received nor sought any US classified information that would threaten the national security of United States. High-ranking officials from FBI and important US military figures confirmed this. A key witness for the prosecution, General James R. Clappen, former Director of Defense Intelligence Agency, who testified as an expert, acknowledged that the accused had not committed espionage against the United States. This and similar other evidence of high ranking US officials knocked out the basis of the charge of conspiracy to commit espionage.

In the trial not a single witness appeared to uphold the charge nor was a single piece of evidence that could link the accused with the alleged crime of conspiracy to commit espionage was produced. In criminal jurisprudence under every jurisdiction including in the United States, the law of espionage is clear. Any information that is generally available to the public at large cannot form the basis of a charge or prosecution for espionage. They must seek or receive information which is secret, confidential or classified the leakage or disclosure of which would jeopardize the national security. It is not each and every information. The information sought or received must impinge on and be damaging to national security. It must not be common knowledge. It has to be information which is in the nature of official secret. It is the disclosure of gathering of such secret information which may constitute an offence of espionage. The very essence of the offence is official secret information disclosure or which is harmful to national security.

The jury, all residents of Miami who were either sympathetic to the anti Cuba activities in Miami or were scared stiff of retaliation from the local volatile, and violent anti-Cuban groups, in the event of the jury or any member of the jury taking a position not in conformity with the wishes of the anti-Cuban terrorist groups. The threats from these groups were not veiled or discreet but were open and terrifying. There were constant intimidating demonstrations outside the court during the entire trial. To scare the members of the jury the license plates of their cars were photographed. The newspapers and the electronic media in Miami constantly campaigned against the Cuban five.

In this background there is no wonder that within a short time the jury came out with a unanimous verdict declaring each of the five accused guilty of each and every charge against them.

Ms. Lenand, the Miami Federal Judge who was assigned this case imposed harsh and long sentences against all the five. She ordered for Gerardo Hernandez, two life sentences plus 15 years; for Ramon Labanino, a life sentence plus 18 years; for Fernando Gonzalez, 19 years in prison; for Rene Gonzalez, 15 years in prison; and for Antonio Guerrero, a life sentence plus 10 years. This again was not surprising. What else could one expect from Judge Ms. Lenard, who while turning down the request of the defense to hold the trial outside Miami, declared to the press that, “this trial will be much more interesting than any TV program.”

Against their conviction and sentence the five accused have filed their appeals before the 11th circuit Court of Appeal. The appeals have been argued on March 10, 2004 and the judgment is awaited.

The grounds on which the appeals are based are sound in law. It is obvious that the five Cubans could not and did not receive a fair trial in Miami. In the interest of justice it was incumbent on the trial court to accept the motion of the accused to shift the trial outside of Miami. Moreover the evidence was clear and unambiguous that there was no conspiracy to commit the murder by Gerardo Hernandez of the four persons in the two planes shot down. Also the acts of a sovereign state in protecting its air space could not in law be a charge against an individual accused who was nowhere near the site of shooting down the aircraft. There was no premeditation to commit the crime. Similarly the change of conspiracy to commit espionage was not proved as they had neither sought nor received any secret information. And to top it all, the sentences awarded are excessive and disproportionate.

However, it is important to note that the United States Attorney had vigorously contended that the Cubans who were accused of conspiracy to spy for the Cuban Government could get a fair trial in Miami and opposed all their motions to move the trial outside Miami. He had contended that Miami was an "extremely heterogeneous, diverse and politically non-monolithic metropolitan area" and that the five Cubans could get a fair trial and full justice in Miami. The self same US Attorney who had persuaded the Court to deny a change of Venue, did a volta face a year later. He himself asked for a change of venue in a civil case wherein allegations of employment discrimination by INS against Latinos were made. He based his motion on the same grounds, that the Cuban five had cited in support of their motion to shift the trial outside Miami. It is on that very basis that the US Attorney argued to demonstrate community prejudice that made a fair trial in Miami impossible. The US Attorney not only relied on the same facts he had in the case of Cuban five rejected as of no consequence but also relied on the same case law which he had termed inapplicable (Pamplin v. Mason, 364F 2nd 1 (5th Cir. 1968). How could the US Attorney make a mockery of the judicial system by taking contradictory positions ignoring his duty and obligation as a public prosecutor, to ensure fair trial and equal justice to all? It is a travesty of justice that when accused who were admittedly agents of the Cuban Government charged with conspiracy to commit espionage and murder contended that they would not get a fair trial in Miami, the US Attorney argued it was possible for them to get justice in Miami but when the defendant in a civil suit is the Attorney General of the United States charged with discrimination in an employment case, which is only remotely connected with Cuba, the US Attorney argues it was "virtually impossible. This contradictory position of the US Government is a clearly deceptive and establishes the case of the five Cubans that they could not and did not get a fair trial in Miami.

The National Lawyer Guild, a representative organization of US Attorneys and an affiliate of the IADL has filed an amicus curie brief before the 11th Circuit Court of Appeal duly adopted and supported by the International Association of Democratic Lawyers pleading for a new trial at a venue outside Miami where the Cubans can be expected to get justice. The amicus brief is before the Court of Appeal. The International Association of Democratic Lawyers has members in over 96 countries and is in Consultative status with ECOSOC of United Nations and representatives at UNESCO and UNICEF.

As a token of their solidarity and in the interest of justice and fair trial the representatives of these and large number of other organizations of lawyers and social activists attended, as observers, the hearing of the Appeal on March 10, 2004.

The case of the five Cubans has raised important questions

of law for which the legal community across the world seeks an answer for the US justice delivery system. Is it not a duty and obligation of a national of sovereign country to safeguard his/her country and its people? It is in response to this patriotic duty that in times of danger to national security the young men and women line up to join the armed force to defend their country. Could it by itself be considered as an offence by other countries? No, this by itself can never be an offence under any law. Similarly if for the sake of defense of his/her country against terrorist machinations and attacks, and to safeguard its people, one is required to penetrate into illegal terrorist outfits to gather intelligence, what offence do they commit? They commit no offence whatsoever. In fact here too they are only discharging their patriotic duty. Their offence can only be if during the course of their duty they violate any law of the land. Gathering information on the terrorist plans of activities against one's country is a patriotic duty and not an offence. Moreover there is no other way one can fight terrorism. It is not a battle between two hostile armies. They are not face-to-face. The terrorist strikes have an element of surprise, disguise and deceit. They generally hit where one may least expect an attack. Often they hit soft targets. One way to prevent and frustrate their attack is to have advance information about the nature and source of attack. This is now the accepted methodology of all anti—terrorist operations. US, UK and all the countries of the world seek to do it in an attempt to safeguard their people. This is not and cannot be an offence of espionage particularly when one is not seeking any government intelligence and only infiltrating terrorist outfits.

Can an action of a sovereign independence country in exercise of its right to safeguard its borders, territorial waters and air space be considered as an offence? One may be an informant about an impending attack or incursion but interception or shooting down of such planes is an act of a sovereign State. No one can be heard to say that in the process, the informant has conspired to commit murder. Any such charge is a gross negation of law and hits at the basic sovereign right of an independent State. It would be a gross violation of international law and of an inherent right of a State to defend itself.

In every criminal trial it is a basic principle of law that the accused must get full opportunity to defend oneself at a fair trial before an independent judiciary. If the venue where trial is scheduled has a vitiated or charged atmosphere, against the accused due to some prejudice against them or is biased in favor of the prosecution, can a fair trial is possible? How in such an atmosphere accused can be expected to effectively defend themselves?

The legal community around the world is watching with great concern the outcome of the Appeals. They seek an answer to the legal issues that arise in these cases and are agitating their minds.

The five Cubans have not only done a patriotic duty in seeking to protect Cuba and its people. These young men have put at stake everything, that they hold dear so that their fellow Cubans could be safe and live in peace. They have challenged terrorism in its own den. They took the fight against terrorism to where terrorism is because they were convinced that it is the only effective way to fight terrorism. They have faced worst form of inhuman treatment, deprivation and degradation during the last six years of their incarceration with courage and supreme confidence. They are the real fighters against terrorism and they shall win.

CHAPTER FOURTEEN

RICARDO ALARCON

Ricardo Alarcon was born in Havana in 1937. Doctor in Philosophy and Humanities from Havana University, he was President of the Federación Estudiantil Universitaria (FEU), permanent ambassador to the United Nations, and Minister of Foreign Affairs.

Since 1993, he is the President of the Cuban Parliament and he is the author of several studies concerning U.S. Cuban relations and the role of democracy in Socialism.

He is undoubtedly the best Cuban specialist on U.S. foreign policy towards his country.

The Cuban Five: An Evidence of U.S. Terrorism Against Cuba

Transcription of a speech by Ricardo Alarcón, President of the Cuban Parliament, during a public hearing on May 10th, 2004.

Espionage is the search for secret data or information of a government. There was no espionage in this case unless the United States considers these terrorist groups a part of its government. If this were the case, the accusation would be right to a certain extent but they should then lift their cloak of hypocrisy and recognize it. The truth is that, for the US administration, these terrorist groups are part of the system like the Education Department, the Health Department or any other. After all, they treat them with a lot of deference. They have enjoyed so much support from the Federal Government that they publicly acknowledge them as if they were a part of the American system.

First of all, I want to express our recognition for your participation here today, the representatives of the diplomatic corps and members of different social organizations and Cuban institutions. Of course, I don't have to say that, as always, we are proud to have with us the members of the families of our five compatriots. I also want to greet a group of Cuban students from the University of Havana Law School who have been very active and in the promotion of the solidarity we need in this cause.

Likewise, I want to give a special welcome to a group of US students who are here visiting our country and we hope we will have many more come and see us. Hopefully, the arbitrary restrictions imposed by the current US administration to cut academic ties and exchanges will come to an end.

For very clear reasons, I'm sure that these young Americans that we have with us today have not heard much about the case of the Five before they came to our country—I see some of them nodding. The most important thing of the issue we are analyzing in this meeting has to do with the most basic rights of these young Americans and the youth of that country. They have the right to live in a sane society. They have the right not to be victims of terrorism or the hypocrisy of those who send them to fight in unjust and unnecessary wars in the name of the struggle against terrorism when, actually, it is the current administration and those in power who are responsible for some of the worst terrorist acts that have taken place in our continent.

And that is the main reason for which it is so difficult to make the case of our five comrades known in the United States. They were arrested, charged, tried and have been punished for the last five years only because they acted against terrorist groups that operate with total impunity inside the United States. This impunity that terrorists enjoy in the US should also be aired and made known to the public.

Leonard [Weinglass] mentioned some of the cases that the US media covers everyday: the trial against Martha Stewart, Michael Jackson or a famous basketball player. They speak of anything but the case of the Five, which clearly proves that the United States is a country governed by a group of people who not only ignore international law and people's aspirations for peace and promotes war everywhere, but hypocritically do it in the name of an alleged opposition to terrorism.

The young Americans here probably don't know who Orlando Bosch is because they don't live in Miami. If they lived there they could see him on TV and they would probably find out about the numerous details of his long career as a terrorist. This man is a terrorist according to US standards. It's not that I say it but the US Justice Department, the body with the authority to do that.

Weinglass was speaking of my address to the UN Security Council where I showed—and it was published—the statement by the US Justice Department. According to that document, Orlando Bosch not only is a terrorist but he is the most well known terrorist of the Western Hemisphere. However, he is not in jail. He is not being punished. Every time he feels like it, he talks on TV in Miami.

Probably, you have not heard of Carlos Muñiz Varela either. He was a young man who was born in Cuba but who became an American citizen. He lived in Puerto Rico and 25 years ago he was killed there in cold blood. There was just one problem: the authorities investigating the case could not find the killers. They only knew, because it was published, that it had been planned by an organization called CORU, a terrorist group whose members were supposedly unknown at that time and, so, no one knew the names of those who had Carlos killed.

Now we know. I saw it. Any Cuban living on the island

knows it—it was shown on TV—from Orlando Bosch's interview when he said, among many other things, that he was the head of CORU. That is, 25 years after the murder of Carlos Muñiz Varela, the problem was solved for the FBI. Supposedly, they could never charge anyone for the crime because they didn't know who the head of CORU was.

Well, the head of the group that took responsibility for the murder has identified himself. Does a crime go away after 25 years? Can anybody boast of being a terrorist in our world today? In a country where hundreds of young people have died in a war that, they say, is part of the struggle against terrorism?

Well, what is the FBI doing? Why don't they ask Bush Sr.? Why don't they arrest him and interrogate him? Do you know why they can't do it? Because the father of the current US president, that at that time was President too, pardoned Bosch. He ignored the Justice Department and simply sent him home. But he didn't stay home quietly: he went on television shows and made public declarations and now he even openly heads an organization... As a result, other American youngsters like Carlos live under the permanent threat of a terrorist or a murderer with such privileged connections.

THE ELIÁN GONZALEZ CASE

Approximately four years ago, some important events related to the judicial process of the Five were taking place in Miami. It was one of the longest and most delayed trials in US history. There were many months of pre-trial litigation about issues like the trial's venue, for instance. The defense team presented several motions to have the trial moved out of Miami.

Four years ago, between April and May, Miami became a very familiar city for all Americans because very unusual things took place there. A five-year-old boy was kidnapped. He was shown on TV every day. The kidnappers did not hide. They were in Miami and they refused to comply with the decision of the federal government that had said the boy should return to his father. Only in Miami could a group of criminals say: “Ok, but no, we don’t feel like doing that.” They didn’t say it protected by the darkness of the night but in broad daylight and in front of television cameras and no one, no authority, could make them comply with that fair and simple decision that was made based on American laws. A judge could not make them comply either when he ruled that the boy should be with his father. The family holding the boy said: “No, we are in Miami and law does not work here and we do as we please. We are in Miami.”

When the federal government asked the local authorities to cooperate in implementing the law, in public statements the City Mayor and the Chief of Police said they would not cooperate with the FBI. It appeared that Miami had separated itself from the Union. Finally, the federal government had to carry out an operation in April. They sent forces to the place where the boy was being kept—they surrounded several houses with heavily armed officers—and rescued him. What did the Mayor and the Chief of Police say? Did they welcome the decision by the federal government? No. Instead, they threatened to set the city on fire. All the American people witnessed the violence, the riots and saw them stamping and even burning the American flag.

In those same days, the federal government, through the Attorney General’s Office, was denying the defense team of our five compatriots their petition to move the trial out of Miami, to Fort Lauderdale, only around 30 miles away in the same southern district. The lawyers didn’t even ask to move it out of the state, but just to another city in Florida, in the same district even, only half an hour away from Miami.

The Government said no, that the trial had to be held in Miami. And Miami—under the risk of being destroyed and set on fire by those people who did what no one ever did in any American city—was a cosmopolitan, marvelous and ideal city for the US government to judge these five men without any problem? Is it that everyone forgot the Miami of Elián's kidnapping? Has anyone tried to link these things, the Elián case and the government's denial of the defense petition to move the trial 30 miles away from Miami?

Weinglass recalled that one year after the end of the trial, this same government was accused in a trial that indirectly had to do with the Elián case. However, in this case, the government said they were taking the case to Fort Lauderdale because it could not take place in Miami where a fair trial could not be had.

Is there any better evidence than this behavior of the attorney's office in Florida that in May or June 2001 said that Miami could host impartial discussions about any topic related to Cuba but in June 2002 they thought completely differently.

THEY WERE NOT CHARGED WITH ESPIONAGE

The Five are often presented as spies but the Government did not even charged them with espionage. They presented an accusation for "conspiracy to commit espionage" against three of them. They did not even charge the five with this accusation. At the same time, the Government recognized that there was no espionage or any classified information involved. Generals and security specialists, under oath, testified as witnesses and all of them made it clear that there was nothing of espionage in the case. They recognized that the Five had tried to discover the plans of the terrorist groups in Miami.

Espionage is the search for secret data or information of a government. There was no espionage in this case unless the United States considers these terrorist groups a part of its government. If this were the case, the accusation would be right to a certain extent, but they should then lift their cloak of hypocrisy and recognize it. The truth is that, for the US administration, these terrorist groups are part of the system like the Education Department, the Health Department or any other. After all, they treat them with a lot of deference. They have enjoyed so much support from the federal government that they act as if they were a part of the American system.

However, it is not legal according to the law, and it should not be acceptable that someone be in prison for having acted, not against the Government and the law, but against terrorists and criminals. And the FBI should have acted against those criminals, and comply with their duty and their obligation to defend American families, instead of acting against these five heroes that were fighting terrorism.

No one has said it, but it would be interesting to make some kind of parallel evaluation of how events developed at that time. While our comrades were in solitary confinement, others were in an airport of South Florida preparing a lethal attack against the American people and the FBI was completely ignorant. That attack would be on September 11, 2001, against the Twin Towers of New York. While our compatriots were falsely accused with charges that had to do with aviation, they could not see those others training to kill Americans. But actually the FBI does not chase terrorists. It protects them.

American youth have the right to demand coherence and consistency from their authorities. At the moment, several US senators have done it. They have asked several questions of the government and we will see what answer they receive. For example, let's take the role of the Office for the Control of Foreign Assets, which belongs to the Treasury Department—the one that enforces the blockade against Cuba—and that should enforce all economic sanctions and control the financial transactions related to terrorism. They don't understand why this office has only four employees working against al-Qaeda, but they have two dozens to enforce the restrictions against Cuba. Are these the US priorities? Why are there more bureaucrats going after you, Americans, than after the murderers? How can anyone explain that? So, that question is there. Several senators have made it. I imagine that at some point they will have to explain.

DISQUALIFICATION

If the venue was the least conceivable place for a fair trial, then it was logical that unusual things could happen as those that happened. I am sure the Gerardo Hernández is the only person in the world condemned to two life sentences and one of them, for something that he was not even accused of in the moment of sentencing. I mean, the Government originally charged him, but during the trial the prosecution had to recognize, as they did in writing on May 25, 2001, that they could not prove this charge and they asked for a modification to the charge. (Remember that, according to the American law, the jury has to find the defendant guilty beyond any reasonable doubt).

Can you imagine twelve people who didn't have any doubts in condemning someone, even though the prosecutor had acknowledged in writing that they could not prove the accusation? There was a total doubt, it was very questionable, and I'll quote what the prosecutor said, the US Attorney General's Office:

"In the light of the evidence presented in the trial, this constitutes an insuperable obstacle for the United States and will probably result in a failure of the accusation in this charge as it poses an insurmountable barrier for this Prosecution."

This was a document that the jury read. And none of the jurors had any reasonable doubt? On the contrary, they found the Five guilty of something that no one was accusing them of. I doubt that there is any person in the world serving a life sentence for something for which they were not accused.

Something is missing that is the key to explain the twisting and the hiding of the truth in this case. Their sentences were not the only ones they received. There is another strange additional punishment and I will quote from the trial transcript:

"The defendant is prohibited from associating with or visiting specific places where individuals or terrorist groups are or visit." (Page 45 corresponding to the Court session of December 14, 2001.)

They included in the sentence a memo written by the US Government, presented before the court, to impose an additional sanction on them. They asked for their "incapacity" in the case of two of our comrades who have American citizenship, René and Antonio—in the other three cases they solve the problem by expelling them from the country after they do their time. This simply means that they cannot do what they used to do. They want to prevent them from learning about other terrorist plans.

Somebody could have thought that including such a clause in René's sentence was an exaggeration or an error of the US Government, but two weeks later, when sentence was read against Antonio, it was repeated. And this "disqualification" demand was so important that the Judge insisted, orally and in written form, that after Antonio fulfilled his sentence—one life plus ten years—he had to comply with this clause: "The defendant is prohibited from associating with or visiting specific places where individuals or terrorist groups are or visit".

December 2001. You surely remember what had happened three months earlier in New York and in American society in general. How many times did Mr. Bush say that he who shelters a terrorist is as guilty as the terrorist himself? Isn't this administration as guilty as the murderers and terrorists it shelters? He repeated this line constantly. However, he who punishes Americans, he who protects and shelters terrorists on US territory, is not as guilty as the terrorist himself? Maybe this will help you understand why it is so difficult for Americans to learn the truth and to understand this case.

Right now there is a scandal in the US regarding the treatment of prisoners in Iraq and the tortures implemented by US and British forces. In England, they knew something since last January and some materials were published in several daily newspapers, including the articles of Robert Fisk that appeared in Mexico (La Jornada) and also in Cuba (Juventud Rebelde). But only now is the information is available for the American people. The International Red Cross affirms that they warned the US government about what was happening in those prisons from February to December 2003.

Someday, much more will be known of the truth about our five compatriots. Someday, Americans will be able to read about what their government said in defense of terrorism in a courtroom in Miami. Someday they will know about the indescribable cruelty and torture they have imposed on these five men and against their mothers, wives and daughters. Someday the US public will find out. It doesn't matter that the powerful groups that control the media in the US continue trying to avoid reporting on the case. If the only way to have something published about the Five is through paid ads in important newspapers—like that of The New York Times last March—we will continue to do it and someday they will know what happened.

What is certain is that we will continue fighting and we will not tire. What we have accomplished thus far is not enough and it gives us no right to rest a minute because our five comrades and their families do not rest, and they are suffering this situation with courage and honor, for us, for our right to live in dignity and also for you, American youth, for the American people, for your right to live and know the truth.

It is our duty, Cubans and those who are not Cubans, to let

the world know about this situation and to let them know who the Five are: men whose altruism is an expression of the best virtues developed by our people.

And as our African comrades say: "The struggle continues, victory is certain."

CHAPTER FIFTEEN

GIANNI MINA

Born in Torino in 1938, Gianni Minà is a world-famous journalist who realized many documentaries for RAI (Italian Radio TV) dealing with culture, sport, and international affairs. He interviewed, among others, Gabriel García Márquez, Jorge Amado, David Alfaro Siquieros, Federico Fellini, Robert De Niro, Muhammad Ali, the Beatles, Sergio Leone, and Fidel Castro.

Collaborator of the Italian daily *La Repubblicca*, Minà regularly writes in newspapers and magazines all around the world.

A Story Covered up by the Information Transnationals

When Five Cubans unmask US State Terrorism

The affair of the five Cubans imprisoned in the USA for the last six years—and sentenced to very heavy jail terms for infiltrating the terrorist headquarters organizing attacks on Cuba from Florida for decades and causing the death of three thousand people—is more and more worrying. An attorney in Miami, Catherine Hueck Miller, has made a clumsy attempt at the time of writing to reply to the insidious questioning by the judges of the XI Federal Appeal Court based at Atlanta Georgia, with jurisdiction over legal controversies raging in the State of Florida. These tertiary judges, who have to clear the doubts surrounding the sentences imposed in 2001 by the Miami Court against the five defendants, René González, Fernando González, Gerardo Hernández, Ramon Labañino and Antonio Guerrero, are trying to understand the basis of the arguments and the logic that found them guilty and sentenced them so heavily. In short, they are trying to excavate one of the darkest corners of US justice. This is why the lawyer, Leonard Weinglass, a former civil rights activist and defender of the "Chicago Eight," including Mumia Abu Jamal and Angela Davies, is not only convinced that the country's fifth and sixth amendments on swift trials and impartial juries (unlikely in Miami where Revolutionary loyalists are involved) have been violated, but also denounces the treatment inflicted on those found guilty: insults, deprivation, unjustified hardships unworthy of the word "democracy," a word inaccurately applied by the George W. Bush government these days.

However, this appeal procedure will not issue in a genuine fresh trial, as would happen in any other developed country in the world, once the violations are verified and the breaches of the law of the land are confirmed, but will consist of an analysis by three XI Federal Appeal Court judges of the possible errors of judgment and law potentially made at the time of the first findings of the Miami court and now due to be corrected.

Yet this is an outrageous story as it springs from an act of disloyalty stubbornly ignored by radio and TV stations and the international press.

When Bill Clinton was still the president, the Cuban Party in Miami, ceaselessly hostile to Fidel Castro for 45 years, had decided that in order to kill off the revolution, which was on an economic upturn after suffering the end of the world, i.e. the end of the socialist market, it was necessary to bring tourism, the leading source of the island's revenue, to its knees. To do this it was necessary to develop terrorist activities to drive away those aiming to spend money in Cuba. This was the world of « Hermanos al Rescate » (Brothers to the Rescue), led by José Basalto who publicly boasted of carrying out acts of aggression against the island and violating its airspace in tiny Cessna aircraft which dropped anti-revolutionary propaganda tracts. Then one day, following twenty-three unanswered diplomatic protest notes, Cuba unfortunately decided, as the US would have done in a similar situation, to shoot two of them down. Meanwhile a climate of constant aggression reigned. Old experts in « dirty wars » in Latin America, Luis Posada Carriles and Orlando Bosch, set up terrorists attacks, but others too were more brazen, like Roby Frometa, who boasted in public press conferences of having carried out assaults and murders in Cuba.

For the first time in such a situation, without ever getting a mention in the international organizations or the information transnationals, the Cuban government decided that it was time to collaborate with the more responsible civil servants in the Clinton administration, going outside the normal diplomatic channels to flag up the achievements of its security agents who exchanged family life for a special, often bitter, life in US society and finding tangible proof of the mafioso activities of certain terrorist organizations in Florida acting against the Revolution.

Through the FBI, President Clinton agreed to cooperate in the elimination of these flashpoints and the embarrassing mafia base, but then the internal politics of the US clearly made him change his mind (had not the Cuban-American National Foundation funded his second campaign quite handsomely?) So when the Havana government, for once not cautious enough, sent the documents, films and recordings confirming the presence of terrorist organizations in the same State which a few years later was to clinch the election for George Bush Junior, instead of arresting these bombers, the US government ordered the arrest of René Gonzalez, Fernando González, Gerardo Hernández, Ramon Labañino and Antonio Guerrero. Having spent 17 months in isolation cells for no reason, the latter had to wait 3 years before being brought to a surrealist and biased trial, in which they were even accused of being indirectly responsible for the shooting down of the two « Brothers to the Rescue » Cessnas.

Over the past few years in Italy I have tried out of respect for my profession to draw the attention of successive governments and political parties to this embarrassing event, especially those who claim to be on the left, as well as the big dailies. But I have not got very far. When the USA perpetrate utterly indefensible actions in the name of morality and justice, there is still unfortunately in my country, fifty years after the US troops helped us to be free from Nazism and Fascism, a kind of psychological and political enslavement which cannot be broken down. There is a kind of myopia blocking out the truth from our view and perpetuating quite unjustifiably an idea of democracy via US culture, transmitted to us in the form of cinema, jazz, great contemporary literature, sport, theatre, avant-garde or Rock'n Roll, all of which come with conquest. But the awareness of this fact, we must note with some bitterness, no longer exists or is virtually extinct.

Probably, indeed, at a time when "preventive war" is supposed to be justifiable, when instead of "invasion," "Liberation" is used, instead of "wiping out" "pacification" and instead of "free exploitation" the euphemism, "free trade," there is, I believe, double-think, a cult of hypocrisy which diverts the gaze, if need be, even of those who claim to be propounding progressive and left-wing views.

It took an editorial in the *Boston Sentinel* by Wayne Smith, the former head of US interests in Havana during the presidency of Jimmy Carter, to reveal last year the double standard behind the Bush administration's policy towards Cuba. The revolutionary government had responded out of the blue with three executions to the attempted subversion (three airliners and the ferry "Regla" sent off course) by the new American chargé d'affaires, James Cason, who has had a budget of $53 million set up to buy an internal opposition. As though democracy could be for sale.

In the 1970s 25 years ago, under Jimmy Carter, Wayne Smith carried out the only genuine effort at peace between Washington and Cuba (it was then reduced to ashes because Reagan, aided by Bush Senior, defeated Jimmy Carter and left him no chance of re-election.) Now that he has become a university researcher, he has rent the vale of hypocrisy censoring the information on the five Cubans condemned to decades of prison for uncovering the terrorism at work within the creases of North American society. The old diplomat writes: "One of the pillars on which the Bush administration's Cuban policy is founded is the assertion that Cuba is a terrorist state harboring hostile intentions towards us. Otherwise, why should we have no relations with Cuba whereas we have them with China, Vietnam and other undemocratic states? The problem is that our present government has not managed to find the slightest suspicion of credible evidence to back its claims. [...] Bush has no interest in dialogue with Cuba, which has, beyond all reasonable doubt, always opposed terrorism. Because it would offend the Florida exiles who support the hard line against Havana, and this sort of thing could make the president's brother lose the swing voters in the elections for State governor. But to maintain that Cuba is a terrorist state undermines our credibility where we most need it, in the fight against the real terrorists."

This is why I went to seek out the details of some private stories about the five lads who have sacrificed themselves for the security of Cuba, at a time when everything goes in the name of a security which actually often disguises a thirst for conquest. I hope the stories will touch the conscience of all people who declare themselves to be democratic.

Just a year and a half ago, for example, at the beginning of April 2003, René González, Fernando González, Gerardo Hernández, Ramón Labañino and Antonio Guerrero, after being arrested in the US for conspiracy and sentenced to ultra-severe penalties, were confined to the "hueco" (the hole, the "dungeon" as

Latin Americans term it). Gerardo Hernández, a graphic designer and cartoonist, was accused of being the head of the group and was due to serve a sentence equivalent to two life sentences plus 15 years.

At the end of 33 months' wait to come to trial, seventeen of them in isolation plus a month in the "hueco," the return of the five Cubans to a normal cell was won thanks to an international campaign joined by a good number of US "liberals," over 100 British Labour MPs and Nadine Gordimer, the South African Nobel Prize winner for literature, but unfortunately no representative of the progressive parties in Italy.

To explain, the "hueco," it is a hole six by two meters, where you stand barefoot, in your underwear; there is no distinction between day and night, as the light is on 24 hours a day; no human contact is available, not even with the jailers, and you have to put up with the continuous howls of inmates kept in this same area for highly aggressive prisoners. Such a description certainly did not fit Gerardo Hernández who, along with his mates, had merely refused at the Miami Trial at the end of 2001, to "cooperate" with the Court. On the eve of the Hearing, he had admitted like the others to being a Cuban Secret Service agent in Florida for the last few years to discover who was organizing terrorist acts against his country. But, in exchange for the promised release, the FBI wanted them to make statements against Cuba, maintaining that their country was a danger to the US and that they had really gone undercover to obtain information about the national security of the USA. Each made an independent decision by this time not to cooperate and their steadfastness astonished the jury. "Why should we attack our country when for years we have been separated from our loved ones and from life itself, for seeking to defend it?" they explained.

The sensational and alarming news made public by these lads' sacrifice was that the USA [ready to justify any action in the name of the war against terrorism and for internal security] was hiding, in the deepest folds of its society, unpunished criminals ready to export political assassination to a country like Cuba, considered a "rogue state" or even linked to terrorism. In one of these terrorist attacks (after the victims had been fishermen, peasants coastguards, part-time soldiers) an Italian citizen, the young businessman Fabio di Celmo, had even been killed on 4th September 1997 at the Hotel Copacabana in Havana. An explosive device had been placed by Cruz, a Salvadorian hired for $10,000 by Luis Posada Carriles who, like his friend, Orlando Bosh, was in the service of the Cuban-American National Foundation in Miami. These partners in crime were also responsible for blowing up an airliner in 1976 off Barbados. Posado Carriles was additionally hired for the assassination plot which took the life of the Chilean Chancellor, Letelier, a former Minister of Foreign Affairs in the Salvador Allende government. No US judge has ever given these people a moment of anxiety. It is easy to imagine the scenario if this event had happened the other way round, i.e. if someone from the island had organized criminal activities in the US. It is sickening to observe the poverty in which Cuba has lived over the last 40 years, not only due to the immoral economic blockade condemned for the eleventh consecutive time by the UN in 2003 (only the US, Israel and the Marshall Islands voted against the removal of economic sanctions) but also because of the media black-out which minimizes these matters and ducks the issue. For instance, so far Gerardo Hernández has been refused visits from his wife, Adriana, in violation of prison rules and the Universal Declaration of Human Rights.

Another story of this type, which might have been written by Luigi Pirandello, involves René González, who also had a US passport as a person born in the United States, the son of a metal worker who had migrated to Chicago and of a Cuban mother whose family came from North Virginia. The grandparents and also the parents, perhaps out of patriotism, decided to return home after the failed Bay of Pigs landing in 1961 by Anti-Castroists supported by the mafia, but cut adrift at the last minute by the Kennedy government. Perhaps this decision cost the chair of Nouvelle Frontière his life. But that is another story.

René, who grew up with the legends of the Revolution, became an aircraft pilot and a flight instructor, while his brother, Roberto, passed a law degree. But one day, to everyone's surprise, René abandoned his wife and daughter, hijacked a crop-spraying plane and went off to the US, where he was greeted as a hero because he had left Fidel Castro's communism behind him.

In Miami, like his four other companions who had arrived in Florida by very different means, he began a new life. They infiltrated terrorist organizations, in particular "Brothers To The Rescue," officially dedicated to the rescue of "balseros" (clandestine immigrants), but really an organizer of bomb plots and the instigator, as already mentioned, of provocative acts such as the systematic violation of Cuban airspace by tourist light aircraft from which, when at low level, they released tracts inciting rebellion. *Brothers To the Rescue* had even begun to invade the airwaves coming from the control towers of the airports of Havana and El Varadero, which endangered the take-off and landing of airliners. At the Miami trial US soldiers like Eugene Carol and civil servants from the Clinton administration like Richard Nunzio, called by the defense, testified that they had warned Basulto that, in the words of one of them, "The Cubans had lost patience" On the other hand, exchanges between the control tower and Opaloca Airport (Florida) do not indicate that Basulto warned his two fellow adventurers, later shot down in the second incursion, of the dangers of the situation.

After six years of sensitive work, René had managed to bring his family over. And so it was that after twelve years he had brought another daughter into the world. But it was also at that same time that the two anxious governments had, through parallel channels, succeeded in setting up dialogue towards a common war on terrorism.

So, in 1998, the Cuban secret services sent reports to the FBI on their group working in Florida to defuse terrorism. But, to everybody's surprise, a few months later these documents were used to arrest the island's five Intelligence sources. René, particularly, had to suffer the insult of finding his wife, Olga, an industrial engineer, threatened and subjected to psychological pressure and economic blackmail to denounce him. Olga herself was detained in the state penitentiary in Fort Lauderdale for refusing to yield to this pressure. Then in 2000 she was deported to Cuba with only her first daughter, not the second, Ivette, born during the couple's stay in the US and now in the care of one of René's great-grandmothers, a US resident.

The first, rather Kafkaesque, trial of the five Cubans was held at the end of 2001 in Miami, with 17 defense lawyers called by the Court refusing the invitation. They feared the repercussions that defending "a Cuban spy" might have on their work in the very state where the anti-Castroist community was most populous and aggressive. Paul McKenna, the duty solicitor for Gerardo Hernández has stated that: "Because of what had happened before, the trial should not, according to our law, have been held in Miami." It should not be forgotten that even McVeigh, the white terrorist and disciple of the seven neo-nazis who was responsible for the massacre at Oklahoma City which killed 200 people, mostly children, won the right to have his trial held in another city not emotionally involved like the one which had suffered the bomb attack.

During the debate in Florida, the prosecution itself had to recognize that the five Cubans had no access to information on national security, so much so that they had to drop charges of spying in favor of « conspiracy to commit acts of espionage », i.e. they were accused of conspiracy to commit a crime. Despite this legal abortion, the jury condemned them to very heavy sentences.

Now the appeal hearing could be adjourned for six months. Leonard Weinglass, Antonio Guerrero's defense lawyer, has stated: "The US government has brought them to trial because they were getting too close to its terrorists." As for the five Cubans' prison conditions before international mobilization on their behalf, these, he added were the worst he had ever seen. More ghastly than those suffered by his former client, Mumia Abu Jamal, the Chicago black journalist leader still awaiting his fate on death row.

I have gone into detail on these stories because they seem to me to explain clearly the policy adopted by George Bush Jr. towards Cuba and they illustrate the whole legal imbroglio surrounding five Cuban lads who agreed to sacrifice part of their live and loves for the safety of their people, who may even have disowned and despised them when they disappeared to the US without warning.

But these extreme events have unfortunately had no effect on other people. People who should have acquainted themselves with them through political ethics or journalistic duty. The *Sun Sentinel*, one of the most widely-read dailies in South Florida, recently revealed that Rodolfo Frometa, one of Washington's most cherished terrorists, is in the State training a group of paramilitaries for a "possible invasion" of Cuba, but the FBI when challenged replied that these groups are not a priority in their work. What do our reformists or the socialist international who are so critical of Cuba or Venezuela think of this unusual way of exporting democracy?

But there is another highly significant story with which I want to close my reflection on this affair. On 15th August 2004 the families of the Cuban victims of the attacks committed by four terrorists with a long history of activities against the Revolution wrote an open letter to Mireya Moscoso, the outgoing President of Panama. In the name of international agreements on the war against terrorism supported and approved by her own government, they respectfully requested her to adopt all measures "necessary to prevent this group of experienced assassins, condemned for an organized attempt on the life of Fidel Castro in November 2000 during the Ibero-American Summit, from escaping from the prison in which they were held."

Furthermore the leader of this handful of gentlemen who happened to have been mopped up by the justice system of the country whose canal divides the American continent in two, was none other than Luis Posada Carriles. As mentioned before, this gentleman, advanced in years but unable to give up terrorist habits applauded by Miami anti-Castroists, blew up a *Cubana de Aviación* airliner over Barbados in 1976 and soon after organized the assassination of Orlando Letelier for DINA, the Chilean Secret Service, and more recently (after other glorious criminal undertakings bankrolled by the CIA and the FBI) sponsored the young Salvadorian, Cruz, who was charged in Havana in 1999 with several "demonstrative acts" with dynamite.

Following this murder, Giustino, the octogenarian father of Fabio di Celmo has spent years vainly seeking a US prosecutor who would agree to investigate those responsible for this strategy of assassination which carried off his son at barely thirty years of age.

Mireya Moscoso, who in 1962 was already married to the then Panamanian President, Arnulfo Arias when he broke off diplomatic relations with Cuba in order to accept an invitation by the Washington government (relations only restored 14 years later by Omar Torrijos), saw no need to reply to this heartfelt appeal. It was an appeal which finished with an undertaking by the victims' family members to « refrain from taking any step to free the terrorists who have plunged our families and our nation into mourning ». And she did not refrain because a month beforehand her Minister for Foreign Affairs had coldly declared that « the terrorists were handed down the sentences which they needed to serve » and that was enough. No, the boorish Mrs. Moscoso ignored this « irrelevant » appeal. Just a few days later, shortly before the swearing in of the new President Elect, Martin Torrijos (son of General Omar Torrijos, who had called for Revolution and had died in a mysterious helicopter accident) she decided to release « on humanitarian grounds » Pedro Ramón, Guillermo Novo, Gaspar Jiménez and of course Luis Posada Carriles, sentenced as recently as in April 2004 to eight years jail. On 26th August they were speedily dispatched in a plane heading for Miami.

The message is clear and disturbing: people and groups who do not fit into the political and economic strategies of the United States and the countries who count, like those in the European Union, are terrorists. These "subversives" must be arraigned irrespective of their rights and of the law of the land. But, surprisingly, there are also the "good terrorists" who act out and assist the hawkish economic groups which in today's world steer the policies of the countries ready to define themselves as "civil and democratic." Did not Ronald Reagan, whom Bush Jr. mourned more than he will probably mourn his own father, call the anti-Sandinista *contras*, the former foot soldiers of the dictator Somoza, "defenders of freedom?"

It is purely because of its point of view that every year the United States hypocritically demands sanctions against Cuba because of the problem of the supposed dissidents. But nothing is mentioned about the three thousand people who have disappeared in the nooks and crannies of the United States security forces because of special anti-terrorist laws, and whose relatives and lawyers have heard nothing from them. The same double standards cause even many left-leaning political parties and supposedly progressive media in Europe to stay silent when the President of Colombia, Alvaro Uribe, scandalously legitimizes Salvatore

Mancuso's paramilitaries by hosting them in the Parliament. These death squads carry out thousands of executions every year and the ex-governor of the province of Antioquia is using them as a crutch to give the impression of governing a country which is now no more than a happy hunting ground for the greediest US multinationals.

Perhaps this long memorandum on the affair of the five Cubans will have made its mark if it helps to reawaken the damaged conscience and pride of the media in the famous free countries, media such as the New York Times, which gave column space to René González, Fernando González, Ramón Labañino and Antonio Gurerrero only after a solidarity committee had bought a one-page advertisement to publicize this dirty, shameful case.

CHAPTER SIXTEEN

NADINE GORDIMER

Novelist, essayist, screenwriter, political activist and champion of the disenfranchised, Nadine Gordimer was born in 1923 in South Africa and rose to world fame for her novels and short stories that stunned the literary world and won her the Nobel Prize for Literature in 1991. In addition to her 12 novels, 10 collections of short stories and essays on topics including apartheid and writing, Gordimer's credits include screenplays for television dramas and the script for the film "Frontiers". Winner of 11 literary awards and 14 honorary degrees, her most recent novel is entitled "The House Gun" and a documentary film entitled "Hanging on a Sunrise".

She was decorated Commandeur de l'Ordre des Arts et des Lettres in France.

Among her most recent novels are *My Son's Story*, *None to Accompany Me*, and *The House Gun*.

Humanity as Justice

If there is any standard of evolution by which we can measure the human being's claim to have become the highest form of life, the ultimate development of superiority above the animal species, it surely must be in the treatment of fellow human beings.

Animals kill one another in the rivalry of survival, the battle for food, and the rivalry for procreation of their species, battling for possession of the females of that species. Humans believe themselves to have evolved beyond such definitions of a destined state of existence; with the one terrible exception, the state of declared war between nations or, even more terrible, of civil war. And in war itself, while the killing of human brother by human brother is the sanctioned object, there are at least international conventions by which if prisoners of war are taken they are to be treated minimally humanly.

This code between creatures representing the highest form of life, the human being, seems not to be observed in times of no, or rather undeclared, war. And it is most blatantly flouted by the world's self-proclaimed greatest democracy and world power, the United States of America. While commandeering a naval base of a foreign sovereign country as a prison for what it has declared its enemy individuals of various nationalities, thereby shifting the immorality off-shore, so to speak, the USA democracy has committed and continues to commit acts flagrantly against all standards of the practices that give men and women the right to claim themselves the highest form of life. There is Guantanamo Bay, and the trial and appeal—both before clearly biased courts—and imprisonment within the USA of the Cuban Five. The conditions in which they are being held would appear too well-known by now to bear repeating, but while these prevail and the validity of the five being sentenced at all remains in question, I believe we cannot confront the people of our world often enough with the appalling facts the Five and their distanced families live with day after day, month after month, now year after year, without action from the populations of the world who yet profess to uphold the justice of humanity.

Why are the Cuban Five restricted in or allowed no access to lawyers? Why are their wives and other members of their families denied visas to visit them? Why do the facts of the degrading and dismal conditions in which they are incarcerated have to be virtually smuggled out in a country in which democracy decrees that justice must be seen to be done wherever it is claimed?

What is the United States afraid of? That admission of wrongdoing will lose its status as Number One Democracy in the world, its marketable export in a trade that does not bear examination? As a somewhat cynical aside, one would think that the unspeakable revelations of the its record in Iraq would mean that the status is already lost and there could be something to be gained by bringing democratic justice and human rights to the Cuban Five. Immediately: it's late.

Many countries can be said not to be innocent of transgressions against our universally accepted human status as the highest form of life, the ultimate development in the evolutionary species. Where the death penalty still is enforced, where there is restriction of freedom of expression, where people lie in prison without trial or, if legally sentenced, exist in inhumanely crowded conditions, no country is exempt, and must look to its own human morality in the treatment of fellow human beings.

But that the most powerful nation in the world, while proclaiming democracy, should seek justification for its actions in the incarceration of the Cuban Five is a shameful betrayal, a travesty of what we have, through centuries, come to define as the basic tenet of humanity. Upon which justice, for anywhere and everywhere, is based.

Forever.

ENDNOTES

WILLIAM BLUM

1. Facts on File, Cuba, the U.S. & Russia, 1960-63 (New York, 1964) pp. 56-8.
2. *International Herald Tribune* (Paris), 2 October 1985, p. 1.
3. *New York Times*, 23 October 1959, p. 1.
4. Facts on File, op. cit., pp. 7-8; New York Times, 19, 20 February 1960; 22 March 1960.
5. *New York Times*, 5, 6 March 1960.
6. David Wise, "Colby of CIA—CIA of Colby," *New York Times Magazine*, 1 July 1973, p. 9.
7. A report about the post-invasion inquiry ordered by Kennedy disclosed that "It was never intended, the planners testified, that the invasion itself would topple Castro. The hope was that an initial success would spur an uprising by thousands of anti-Castro Cubans. Ships in the invasion fleet carried 15,000 weapons to be distributed to the expected volunteers." *U.S. News & World Report*, 13 August 1979, p. 82. Some CIA officials, including Allen Dulles, later denied that an uprising was expected, but this may be no more than an attempt to mask their ideological embarrassment that people living under a "communist tyranny" did not respond at all to the call of "The Free World."
8. Attacks on Cuba:
   a) Taylor Branch and George Crile III, «The Kennedy Vendetta», *Harper's magazine* (New York), August 1975, pp. 49-63
   b) Facts on File, op. cit., passim
   c) *New York Times*, 26 August 1962, p. 1; 21 March 1963, p. 3; *Washington Post*, 1 June 1966; 30 September 1966; plus many other articles in both newspapers during the 1960s
   d) Warren Hinckle and William W. Turner, *The Fish is Red: The Story of the Secret War Against Castro* (Harper & Row, New York, 1981) passim.
9. Branch and Crile, op. cit., pp. 49-63. The article states that there were in excess of 300 Americans involved in the operation, but in "CBS Reports: The CIA's Secret Army," broadcast 10 June 1977, written by Bill Moyers and the same George Crile III, former CIA

official Ray Cline states that there were between 600 and 700 American staff officers.

10 *New York Times*, 26 August 1962, p. 1.

11 John Gerassi, *The Great Fear in Latin America* (New York, 1965, revised edition) p. 278.

12 *New York Times*, 28 April 1966, p. 1.

13 Branch and Crile, op. cit., p. 52

14 *Washington Post*, 21 March 1977, p. A18.

15 Hinckle and Turner, p. 293, based on their interview with the participant in Ridgecrest, California, 27 September 1975.

16 *San Francisco Chronicle*, 10 January 1977.

17 Bill Schaap, "The 1981 Cuba Dengue Epidemic," *Covert Action Information Bulletin* (Washington), No. 17, Summer 1982, pp. 28-31.

18 *San Francisco Chronicle*, 29 October 1980, p.15.

19 *Science* (American Association for the Advancement of Science, Washington), 13 January 1967, p. 176.

20 *Covert Action Information Bulletin* (Washington), No. 22, Fall 1984, p. 35; the trial of Eduardo Victor Arocena Perez, Federal District Court for the Southern District of New York, transcript of 10 September 1984, pp. 2187-89.

21 See, e.g., *San Francisco Chronicle*, 27 July 1981.

22 *Washington Post*, 16 September 1977, p. A2.

23 Ibid., 25 October 1969, column by Jack Anderson.

24 Reports of the assassination attempts have been disclosed in many places; see Interim Report: Alleged Assassination Plots Involving Foreign Leaders, The Select Committee to Study Governmental Operations with Respect to Intelligence Activities (US Senate), 20 November 1975, pp. 71-180, for a detailed, although not complete, account. Stadium bombing attempt: *New York Times*, 22 November 1964, p. 26.

25 *New York Times*, 12 December 1964, p. 1.

26 Ibid., 3 March 1980, p. 1.

27 Terrorist attacks within the United States:
a) Jeff Stein, "Inside Omega 7," *The Village Voice* (New York), 10 March 1980

b) *San Francisco Chronicle*, 26 March 1979, p. 3; 11 & 12 December, 1979.

c) *New York Times*, 13 September 1980, p. 24; 3 March, 1980, p. 1.

d) John Dinges and Saul Landau, *Assassination on Embassy Row* (London, 1981), pp. 251-52, note (also includes attacks on Cuban targets in other countries)

e) *Covert Action Information Bulletin* (Washington), No. 6, October 1979, pp. 8-9.

28 The plane bombing:

a) *Washington Post*, 1 November 1986, pp. A1, A18.

b) Jonathan Kwitny, *The Crimes of Patriots* (New York, 1987), p. 379.

c) William Schaap, "New Spate of Terrorism: Key Leaders Unleashed," *Covert Action Information Bulletin* (Washington), No. 11, December 1980, pp.4-8.

d) Dinges and Landau, pp. 245-6. e) Speech by Fidel Castro, 15 October 1976, reprinted in Toward Improved U.S.-Cuba Relations, House Committee on International Relations, Appendix A, 23 May 1977.

The CIA documents: Amongst those declassified by the Agency, sent to the National Archives in 1993, and made available to the public. Reported in *The Nation* (New York), 29 November 1993, p. 657.

29 Dangerous Dialogue: Attacks on Freedom of Expression in Miami's Cuban Exile Community, p. 26, published by America's Watch and The Fund for Free Expression, New York and Washington, August 1992.

30 Ibid., passim. Also see: "Terrorism in Miami: Suppressing Free Speech," *CounterSpy magazine* (Washington), Vol. 8, No. 3, March-May 1984, pp. 26-30; *The Village Voice*, op. cit.; *Covert Action Information Bulletin* (Washington), No. 6, October 1979, pp. 8-9.

31 *New York Times*, 4 January 1975, p. 8.

32 *San Francisco Chronicle*, 12 January 1982, p. 14; *Parade magazine* (*Washington Post*), 15 March 1981, p. 5.

33 *The Village Voice*, op. cit.
34 *The Miami Herald*, November 16, 1997.
35 *Associated Press*, Tampa, Fla., July 16, 1997.
36 *Washington Post*, February 5, 1998, p. 28.
37 Associated Press, February 7, 1999.
38 *Associated Press* (AP), May 11, 2001
39 *US District Court, Southern District of Florida*, case #98-3493, Criminal Complaint, September 14, 1998, "Conclusion" paragraph. Hereafter, "Criminal Complaint".
40 *EFE News Service* (based in Madrid, with branches in the US), March 28, 2001
41 *Miami Herald*, September 18, 1998
42 Criminal Complaint, paragraph 7
43 *New York Times*, 3 March 1980, p. 1
44 *EFE News Service*, March 28, 2001
45 See for example *Miami Herald*, March 28, 2001, p.1B
46 Criminal Complaint, paragraph 7; see also paragraph 26.
47 *Ibid.*, paragraph 19
48 *Miami Herald*, September 23, 1998
49 *Washington Post*, September 15, 1998; *Miami Herald*, September 16, 1998
50 *US District Court, Southern District of Florida*, Case No. 98-721, Second Superseding Indictment, May 7, 1999, Count 2, Section D
51 *Miami Herald*, September 16, 1998
52 *Department of Justice*, Bureau of Justice Statistics, reported to author by John Scalia, statistician at the bureau.
53 *Associated Press*, May 8, 2001
54 *EFE News Service*, March 28, 2001
55 Carl Nagin, "Backfire", *The New Yorker*, January 26, 1998, p.32
56 Jefferson Morley, "Shootdown", *Washington Post Magazine*, May 25, 1997, p.120.
57 *EFE News Service*, February 1, 2001
58 *Ibid.*, March 1, 2001
59 *Associated Press*, March 21, 2001; *Miami Herald*, March 22, 2001

60 *New York Times*, February 26, 1996, p.1

61 *Associated Press*, December 5, 2000

62 *New York Times*, February 26, 1996, p.1. It is not clear from the article whether the transmission was made by the FAA or by BTTR.

63 *The New Yorker*, op. cit., p.34

64 Second Superseding Indictment, see op. cit., Count 3, Section A

65 *The New Yorker*, op. cit., p.33

66 *Newsweek*, March 11, 1996, p.48

67 Jane Franklin, *Cuba and the United States: A Chronological History* (Ocean Press, Australia, 1997), see index under "Planes used against Cuba"; William Blum, *Killing Hope: US Military and CIA Interventions Since World War II* (Common Courage Press, Maine, 1995), Cuba chapter.

68 *Washington Post*, February 27, 1996

NOTES—MICHAEL PARENTI

1 Quoted in William Langer, ed., *An Encyclopedia of World History*, 5th ed. (Boston: Houghton Mifflin, 1980), 1246.

2 For more details on U.S. interventionism in these various places, see my *Against Empire* (San Francisco: City Lights Books, 1995); and my *To Kill a Nation: The Attack Against Yugoslavia* (New York/ London: Verso, 2000).

3 Manuel de Varona, quoted in *New York Daily News*, 8 January 1961.

4 Robert Cirino, *Power to Persuade* (New York: Bantam, 1974); also Victor Bernstein and Jesse Gordon, "The Press and the Bay of Pigs," Columbia University Forum reprint, Fall 1967.

5 *New York Times*, 8 January 1961; *Time*, 13 January 1961.

6 *New York Times*, 8 January 1961.

7 Newsletter, Center for Cuban Studies, 3, winter 1976.

8 Vanessa Arrington's report, Associate Press 12 May 2004.

9 *New York Times*, 5 August 1984.

10 Fidel Castro interviewed in the PBS documentary, *Shadow of a*

Doubt, shown in October 1986.

NOTES—PIERO GLEIJESES

1 Thenjiwe Mtintso, "Speaker's Notes to OSPAAL Celebrations," Havana, Jan. 15, 2004, pp.1-2.
2 Fidel Castro, in "Indicaciones concretas del Comandante en Jefe que guiarán la actuación de la delegación cubana a las conversaciones en Luanda y las negociaciones en Londres (23-4-88)," p. 5, Centro de Información de la Defensa de las Fuerzas Armadas Revolucionarias, Havana (hereafter CIDFAR).
3 Nelson Mandela, July 26, 1991, *Granma* (Havana), July 27, 1991, p. 3.
4 My discussion of the events in 1975-76 is based on my book, *Conflicting Missions: Havana, Washington, and Africa, 1959-1976*, Chapel Hill, 2002. Here, I will cite only the sources of direct quotations. My discussion on 1987-88 is based on my ongoing research on Cuban and US policy toward Angola in the Carter and Reagan years.
5 Robert Hultslander (CIA station chief, Luanda, 1975), fax to Piero Gleijeses, Dec. 22, 1998, p. 3.
6 Anatoly Dobrynin, *In Confidence: Moscow's Ambassador to America's Six Cold War Presidents*, New York, 1995, p. 362.
7 Henry Kissinger, *Years of Renewal*, New York, 1999, p.816.
8 Ibid., p.785.
9 Roger Sargent, *Rand Daily Mail* (Johannesburg), Feb. 17, 1976, p.10.
10 *World* (Johannesburg), Feb. 24, 1976, p. 4.
11 My comment about Carter is based on newly declassified documents from the Jimmy Carter Library in Atlanta. Even though our conclusions differ, I have greatly benefitted from Professor Nancy Mitchell's path-breaking manuscript, "Pragmatic Moralist: Jimmy Carter and Rhodesia."
12 Jannie Geldenhuys, *A General's Story: From an Era of War and Peace*, Johannesburg, 1995, p. 59.

13 Chester Crocker, *High Noon in Southern Africa: Making Peace in a Rough Neighborhood*, New York, 1992.

14 Perkins (US ambassador, Pretoria) to SecState, Apr. 17, 1987, Freedom of Information Act (hereafter FOIA).

15 United Nations Security Council resolution #602 of Nov. 25, 1987.

16 SecState to Amembassy Pretoria, Dec. 5, 1987, FOIA.

17 *Star* (Johannesburg), Jan. 21, 1988, p. 1.

18 "Transcripción sobre la reunión del Comandante en Jefe con la delegación de políticos de Africa del Sur (Comp. Slovo) efectuada en el MINFAR el 29.9.88," p. 16, CIDFAR.

19 See Jorge Risquet in V.I. Vorotnikov, *Havana - Moskvá: pamiatnie godu*, Moscow, 2001, p. 210..

20 Jan Breytenbach, *Buffalo Soldiers: The Story of South Africa's 32 Battalion 1975 - 1993*, Alberton, South Africa, 2002, p. 308.

21 "Conversaciones sostenidas el 26/3/88 entre el compañero Jorge Risquet y el viceministro de relaciones exteriores de la URSS Anatoly Adamishin," pp. 3, 5, enclosed in Risquet to Fidel Castro, March 27, 1988, Archives of the Central Committee of the Communist Party of Cuba, Havana (hereafter ACC).

22 "Conversacion del Comandante en Jefe Fidel Castro Ruz, primer secretario del comité central del Partido Comunista de Cuba y presidente de los Consejos de Estado y de Ministros, con Anatoli L. Adamishin, viceministro de relaciones exteriores de la URSS. Efectuada el día 28 de marzo de 1988," p. 48, ACC.

23 Abramowitz (Bureau of Intelligence and Research, Department of State) to SecState, May 13, 1988, pp. 1-2, FOIA.

24 General Jannie Geldenhuys, Chief of the South African Defence Forces, *Star* (Johannesburg), May 27, 1988, p. 1; Defense Minister Magnus Malan, *Star*, May 17, 1988, p. 1;

25 Quotations from Bureau of Intelligence and Research, Department of State, "Peacemaking in Angola: A Retrospective Look at the Effort," June 10, 1988, p. 4, FOIA; P.W. Botha, Aug. 24, 1988,

26 Republic of South Africa, *Debates of Parliament*, sixth sess., eighth parliament, col. 15508; "Entrevista Dobrynin—Risquet," May 10, 1988, p. 14, ACC.

27 "Entrevista de Risquet con Chester Crocker. 26/6/88, 18:30 horas. Hotel Hyatt, El Cairo," pp. 22-23, 26-27, ACC.
28 Col. Dick Lord, quoted in Fred Bridgland, *The War for Africa: Twelve Months That Transformed a Continent*, Gibraltar, 1990, p.361; CIA, "South Africa—Angola—Cuba," June 29, 1988, FOIA.
29 CIA, "South Africa—Angola—Namibia," July 1, 1988, FOIA.
30 *Die Kerkbode* (Cape Town), July 8, 1988, p. 4 (ed.); *Star*, July 8, 1988, p. 10 (ed.).
31 See "Documento aprobado como resultado de las discusiones militares celebradas en Cabo Verde el 22-23 de julio de 1988," CIDFAR.
32 Amembassy Brazzaville to SecState, Aug. 25, 1988, p. 6, National Security Archive, Washington DC.

NOTES—IGNACIO RAMONET

1 Nelson Mandela, July 26, 1991, *Granma*, July 27, 1991, p. 3.
2 Leycester Coltman, *The Real Fidel Castro*, New Haven, 2003, p. 289.

NOTES—SALIM LAMRANI

1 *Newsweek*, "Special Issue on the 1984 Presidential Election," November/December 1984: 32. (My emphasis)
2 Morris H. Morley, *Imperial State and Revolution: The United States and Cuba, 1952-1986* (Cambridge: Cambridge University Press, 1987), p. 319.
3 Hernando Calvo Ospina & Katlijn Declercq, *Dissidents ou Mercenaires* (Brussels: EPO, 1998), p. 76
4 Jane Franklin, *Cuba and the United States: a Chronological History* (Melbourne, New York: Ocean Press, 1997), pp. 178-79.
5 Jean Solbès. *Le Défi cubain* (Paris: Graphein, 1998), p. 292.
6 Ninoska Pérez Castellón, *Un hombre y su tiempo. El pensamiento político de Jorge Mas Canosa* (Miami: Endowment for Cuban American Studies of the Cuban American National Foundation &

The Jorge Mas Canosa Freedom Fund, July 1998).

7 Office of Cuba Broadcasting, "Radio Marti: Mission," *U.S. International Broadcasting Bureau*, www.martinoticias.com/mision.asp (site consulted 08.14.2004).

8 *Ibid.* ; Nick Grace C. "Radio Marti," Declassified Top Secret, February 8, 1998. www.qsl.net/yb0rmi/marti.htm (site consulted 08.14.2004); Michael Bowman, "U.S. Cuba Broadcasting," Global Security, February 8, 1999. www.globalsecurity.org/intell/library/news/1999/02/990205-cuba1.htm (site consulted 08.14.2004).

9 *Voice Of America*, "Review of Policies and Procedures for Ensuring that Radio Marti Broadcasts Adhere to Applicable Requirements," Audit Report 99-IB-010, June 1999, 1, 3, 5, 13, 15, 17. http://oig.state.gov/documents/organization/7449.pdf (site consulted 08.14.2004); Rui Ferreira, "Director de Radio Martí emplea a sus amigos," *El Nuevo Herald*, March 21, 2002 : 6A.

10 Dan Griswold, "Will U.S. Trade with Cuba Promote Freedom or Subsidize Tyranny?," *Cato Institute Policy Forum*, July 25, 2002, 17. www.cato.org/events/transcript/020725et.pdf (site consulted 08.14.2004).

11 Salim Lamrani, *Cuba face á l'Empire: Propagande, guerre économique et terrorisme d'Etat* (Outremont: Lanctôt, 2005)

12 Salim Lamrani, "Recrudecimiento de la agresión estadounidense contra Cuba," *Rebelión*, June 8, 2004. www.rebelion.org/cuba/040608lamrani.htm (site consulted 08.14.2004).

13 William Schaap, "La Demanda: The People of Cuba vs the U.S. Government" *Third World Traveler*, September-December 1999. www.thirdworldtraveler.com/Latin_America/LaDemanda.htm (site consulted 08.14.2004).

14 Noam Chomsky & Edward S. Herman, *Economie politique des droits de l'homme. La "Washington Connection" et le Fascisme dans le Tiers Monde* (Paris: J.E. Hallier & Albin Michel, 1981), p. 50.

15 Jean-Guy Allard, "On Luis Posada Carriles," *Granma Internacional*, February 28, 2002. www.antiterroristas.cu/index.php?tpl=noticia/anew¬iciaid=144¬iciafecha=2002-09-11 (site consulted 08.14.2004).

16 *New York Times*, "Seventy-Eight Are Believed Killed as Cuban Jetliner Crashes in sea After Blast," October 7, 1976. www.nytimes.com/library/world/americas/100776cubaairliner.html (site consulted 08.14.2004); *New York Times*, "Anti-Castro Extremists Tolerated, if not Encouraged, by Some Latin American Nations," November 15, 1976. www.nytimes.com/library/world/americas/111576cubaailiner.html (site consulted 08.14.2004); David Binder, "Two Nations Report Anti-Castro Exiles Have Plotted Many Terrorists Acts," *New York Times*, October 20, 1976. www.nytimes.com/library/world/americas/102076cuba-ailiner.html (site consulted 08.14.2004).

17 John F. Kerry, "Selections from the Senate Committee. Report on Drugs, Law Enforcement and Foreign Policy Chaired by Senator John F. Kerry," 1988. www.webcom.com/pinknoiz/covert/contracoke.html (site consulted 08.14.2004).

18 *Radio Habana Cuba*, "Giustino di Celmo, père du jeune italien tué dans l'attentat de l'hôtel Copacabana le 4 septembre 1997," 2002. www.radiohc.cu/heroes/frances/testimonios.dicelmo.htm (site consulted 08.14.04).

19 Ann Louise Bardach & Larry Rohter, "Key Cuba Foe Claims Exiles' Backing," *New York Times*, July 12, 1998: 1.

20 *Ibid.*

21 *Ibid.*

22 Ann Louise Bardach & Larry Rohter, "Authorities Knew of Bombing Campaign, Says Cuban Exile," *New York Times*, July 12, 1998: 1, 2, 3. www.nytimes.com/library/world/americas/071298cuba-bombs.html (site consulted 02.03.03)

23 Juan O. Tamayo, "Witness: I Was a Castro Spy in Foundation," *The Miami Herald*, March12, 1999: 1A.

24 Glenn Garvin, "Panama: Exile Says Aim Was Castro Hit," *The Miami Herald*, January 13, 2001: 1A; Glenn Garvin & Frances Robles, "Panama Suspect Has Ties to Dade. Anti-Castro Figure Was Indicted in '76 Milian Case," *The Miami Herald*, November 21, 2001: 1A; John Rice, "Panama: Fidel Steals Show With Death Plot," *The Associated Press*, November 18, 2000; Fernando Martínez & David Aponte, "Anticastristas llegaron a Panamá para

asesinarlo, denuncia Castro," *La Jornada*, November 18, 2000; *El Nuevo Herald*, "Condenan en Panamá a Luis Posada Carriles," April 21, 2004: 23A; *El Nuevo Herald*, "Piden pena máxima contra anticastristas," March 18, 2004: 17A.

25 *El Nuevo Herald*, "Recaudan fondos para exiliados presos en Panamá," April 23, 2004: 17A.

26 *International Herald Tribune*, "Four Cubans Pardoned," August 27, 2004. www.iht.com/articles/535947.html (site consulted 08.27.04); Anita Snow, « Mireya Moscoso indulta a cuatro anticastristas », *El Nuevo Herald*, August 27, 2004. www.miami.com/mld/elnuevo/news/world/cuba/9506952.htm (site consulted 08.27.04).

27 Glenn Kessler, "U.S. Denies Role in Cuban Exile's Pardon," *Washington Post*, August 27, 2004: A18.

28 Ann Louise Bardach & Larry Rohter, "Key Cuba Foe Claims Exiles' Backing," *op. cit.*

29 Rui Ferreira, "Mireya Moscoso indulta a cuatro anticastristas," *El Nuevo Herald*, August 27, 2004 :

30 Alfonso Chardy, Gerardo Reyes & Fabiola Santiago, "Exile Group's Officials Facing Indictment in Anti-Castro Plot," *The Miami Herald*, August 21, 1998: 1A; Frances Robles & Glenn Garvin, "Four Held in Plot Against Castro," *The Miami Herald*, November 19, 2000: 1A.

31 Jean-Guy Allard, "Escándalo de espías para salvar a la FNCA," *Granma Internacional*, June 26, 2001. www.granma.cubaweb.cu/miami5/enjuiciamiento/justicia/0089.html (site consulted 08.13.04).

32 Kirk Nielsen, "Spies in Miami, Commandos in Cuba," *Miami New Times*, July 5, 2001, 2. www.miaminewtimes.com/issues/2001-07-05/metro.html (site consulted 02.03.03).

33 Robert Sheer, "A Startling Tale of U.S. Complicity," *Los Angeles Times*, July 14, 1998: 7.

34 Juan O. Tamayo, "Anti-Castro Plot Seldom Leads to Jail in U.S.," *The Miami Herald*, July 23, 1998: 11A.

35 Mumia Abu-Jamal, "Los Cinco impidieron más de 170 actos terroristas contra Cuba," *Granma Internacional*, January 2, 2003. www.granma.cu/espanol/ene03/juev2/cinco.html (site consulted

08.14.2004).

36 Paul McKenna, "Nunca hubo prueba alguna de que los Cinco Patriotas fueran a causa daño a los EE.UU," *Granma Internacional*, August 15, 2002). www.granma.cubaweb.cu/miami5/espanol/00208.html (site consulted 08.14.2004); Leonard Weinglass, "El apoyo internacional realza la importancia del caso ante los tribunales, dice Weinglass" *Agencia de Información Nacional*, January 18, 2003. www.injusticia_en_miami.cubaweb.cu/coberturacompleta/2003/ene2103weiglass.htm (site consulted 08.14.2004); Simon Wollers, "Rob Miller of the Cuba Solidarity Campaign in Britain: We Question the Judicial Process of the Five," *Antiterroristas.cu*, November 4 2002. www.antiterroristas.cu/index.php?tlp=noticia/anew¬iciaid=558¬iciafecha=2002-12-10 (site consulted 08.14.2004); Simon Wollers, "National Jury Project: El juicio de Miami quitó cualquier posibilidad a los acusados cubanos," *Antiterroristas.cu*, December 2002). www.antiterroristas.cu/index.php?tlp=noticia/anew¬iciaid=612¬iciafecha=2002-12-23 (site consulted 08.14.2004); Jean-Guy Allard, "Escándalo de espías para salvar a la FNCA," *Granma Internacional*, June 26, 2001). www.granma.cubaweb.cu/miami5/espanol/0089.html (site consulted 08.14.2004).

37 www.freethefive.org/whoare.cfm "Who are the Five" (site consulted 08.14.2004).

38 Pablo Alfonso & Rui Ferreira, "Cae red de espionaje de Cuba. Arrestan a 10 en Miami," *El Nuevo Herald*, September 15, 1998: 1A.

39 Wilfredo Cancio Isla, "Bush pide la rápida restricción de viajes a Cuba," *El Nuevo Herald*, October 14, 2003: 4A.

40 United Nations Economic Commission for Latin America and the Caribbean (ECLAC), *The Cuban Economy. Structural Reforms and Economic Performance in the 1990s* (Mexico: United Nations, December 6, 2001), p. 184.

41 Robert Merle, *Moncada: premier combat de Fidel Castro* (Paris: Robert Laffont, 1965), p. 34.

NOTES—LEONARD WEINGLASS

Professor of Sociology and Anthropology and Director of the Cuban Research Institute at Florida International University

1 Poll taken in 2000 by Kendra H. Brennan of KHB Consulting, Inc., at the request of the defense.

2 Interview with Diaz-Balart on Miami Television, TV Channel 41, March 22, 2004

3 See p. 15 of the Initial Brief of Appellant Luis Medina III.

4 Ibid, p. 16

5 Ibid

6 See p. 3 of the Appeal filed for Gerardo Hernandez

7 It is interesting to note that the FAA described Basulto's conduct in continuing the flight even after being warned as "irresponsible," and his pilot's license was revoked.

8 Hernandez appeal, op. cit., p. 21